THE PRENTICE HALL REGENTS

PREP SERIES for the TOEFL® TEST

FOUR PRACTICE TESTS

Lin Lougheed

Instructional Design International, Inc.

TOEFL® is a registered trademark of Educational Testing Service (ETS).
No affiliation between ETS and Prentice Hall Regents is implied.

Prentice Hall Regents
Englewood Cliffs, New Jersey 07632

Lougheed, Lin. 1946–
   The Prentice Hall Regents prep series for the TOEFL test / Lin
Lougheed
        p.   cm.
   Originally published in 1 v. : Regents/Prentice Hall TOEFL prep
book. 2nd ed. Englewood Cliffs, N.J. : Regents/Prentice Hall. ©1992
   Contents: [1] Four practice tests – – [2] Grammar skills builder – –
[3] Listening skills builder – – [4] Vocabulary skills builder – –
   ISBN 0-13-870015-X (1). – – ISBN 0-13-100637-1 (2). – – ISBN
0-13-100652-5 (3). – – ISBN 0-13-100660-6
  1. Test of English as a Foreign language– –Study guides.
  2. English language—Textbooks for foreign speakers. I. Lougheed.
Lin, 1946– Regents/Prentice Hall TOEFL prep book. II. Title.
PE1128.L65 1995
428'.0076—dc20   94–25977
                                                 CIP

Acquisitions editor: Nancy Baxer
Director of production and manufacturing: David Riccardi
Editorial production/design manager: Dominick Mosco
Editorial/production supervision: Christine McLaughlin Mann
Production coordinator: Ray Keating

Cover design coordinator: Merle Krumper
Cover design: Wanda España

© 1995 by **PRENTICE HALL REGENTS**
Prentice-Hall, Inc.
A Simon & Schuster Company
Englewood Cliffs, New Jersey 07632

TOEFL test directions taken from Test of English as a Foreign Language, Educational Testing
Service, © 1993. Reprinted by permission of Educational Testing Service.

Permission to reprint TOEFL materials does not constitute review or endorsement by
Educational Testing Service of this publication as a whole or of any other testing information
it may contain.

Printed in the United States of America

10 9 8 7 6 5 4 3 2 1

ISBN   0-13-870015-X

Printed on Recycled Paper

Prentice-Hall International (UK) Limited, London
Prentice-Hall of Australia Pty. Limited, Sydney
Prentice-Hall Canada Inc., Toronto
Prentice-Hall Hispanoamericana, S.A., Mexico
Prentice-Hall of India Private Limited, New Delhi
Prentice-Hall of Japan, Inc., Tokyo
Simon & Schuster Asia Pte. Ltd., Singapore
Editora Prentice-Hall do Brasil, Ltda., Rio de Janeiro

CONTENTS

Preface

The *Prentice Hall Regents Prep Series for the TOEFL® Test*: Structure and Written Expression Skills Builder will help you become familiar with the two types of questions used in the Structure and Written Expression section of the TOEFL The format of the questions is similar to the actual format of the real TOEFL. By reviewing the English grammar targeted in this book, you will improve both your test-taking skills and your knowledge of English.

The complete *Prentice Hall Regents Prep Series for the TOEFL® Test* contains hundreds of listening, reading, and writing activities that are designed to help you improve your score on the TOEFL. When you finish the Four Practice Tests, you may want to study for the other sections of the TOEFL.

Prentice Hall Regents Prep Series for the TOEFL® Test

Listening Skills Builder	ISBN: 0-13-100652-5
Vocabulary and Reading Comprehension Skills Builder	ISBN: 0-13-100660-6
Grammar Skills Builder	ISBN: 0-13-100637-1

Acknowledgments

I wish to acknowledge and thank the many teachers and students around the world whose advice and comments shaped this revision. I am especially appreciative of the insightful suggestions of Dr. Richard Kimble, California State University, Hayward, and Kathy Prout and Cheryl Sparks, Martinez Adult School, Martinez, California.

HOW TO BEGIN

First look over this entire book. Notice there are answer sheets and explanatory answers for the Structure and Written Expression Targets in the back of the book. Study the potential problems for each target and then practice the strategy and skill-building sections. Don't forget to do the Grammar Review exercises.

❏ HOW TO OBTAIN THE ACCOMPANYING TAPES AND OTHER TOEFL BOOKS

n the United States

By mail or phone from institutional customers:
Please forward your purchase order on official letterhead and mail to:

Prentice Hall Regents
Order Department
200 Old Tappan Road
Old Tappan, NJ 07675
1-800-223-1360

All orders from individuals must be sent to:

Prentice Hall Regents
Mail Order Processing
200 Old Tappan Road
Old Tappan, NJ 07675
Individuals without accounts who wish to place orders may call Mail Order Billing at (201) 767-5937.

utside the United States

Contact your nearest Prentice Hall International representative.

Canada
Please forward your purchase order on official letterhead and mail to:
Kedre Murray
Prentice Hall Canada
ESL
1870 Birchmount Road
Scarborough, Ontario M1P2J7
Tel: (416) 293-36221

United Kingdom, Europe, Africa & Middle East
Norman Harris
Prentice Hall International (UK) Ltd.
Campus 400
Maylands Avenue
Hemel Hempstead
Herts., HP2 7EZ England
Tel: (442) 881-900
Telex: 82445
FAX: (442) 882-099

Japan
Harry Jennings
Prentice Hall of Japan
Nishishinjuku KF Bldg. 602
8-14-24, Nishishinjuku
Shinjuku-ku, Tokyo 160
Japan
Tel: (03) 3365-9002
Fax: (03) 3365-9009
Telex: 6502958590

Mexico, Central America & South America
Simon & Schuster International
Regents/Prentice Hall
International Customer Service Group
200 Old Tappan Road
Old Tappan, New Jersey 07675
U.S.A.
Tel: (201) 767-4990
Telex: 990348
FAX: (201) 767-5625

All Other Asian Orders
David Fisher
Simon & Schuster (Asia) Pte. Ltd.
24 Pasir Panjang Road
#04-31 PSA Multi-Storey Complex
Singapore 0511
Tel: 2789611
Telex: RS 37270
FAX: 2734400

Australia & New Zealand
Simon & Schuster (Australia) Pty. Ltd.
P.O. Box 151
7 Grosvenor Place
Brooksvale, N.S.W. 2100
Australia
Tel: (02) 939-1333
Telex: PHASYD AA 74010
FAX: (02) 938-6826

Introduction

❏ THE TOEFL: WHAT IS IT?

The TOEFL, the Test of English as a Foreign Language, measures the English proficiency of non-native English speakers. It tests their ability to understand spoken English, recognize correct grammatical constructions, identify synonyms, and comprehend reading passages.

The test is divided into three sections. Each section is timed. The chart below gives a general outline of the exam. The exact format of the exam may vary; the number of questions and the time given occasionally differ from test to test. The TOEFL uses several different forms, some of which may include experimental questions. These questions look like the other test questions but will not be counted in your score. The experimental questions and the time allotted for them are in parentheses in the chart.

❏ THE TOEFL: WHO NEEDS IT?

Most American colleges and universities require evidence of a student's English language proficiency for admission. The TOEFL is one of the tests given for this purpose. The TOEFL, however, is only one of the criteria for admission. A satisfactory score on the TOEFL does not guarantee admission to a university.

Section	Questions	Minutes
Section One **Listening Comprehension** Part A: Short Statements Part B: Short Conversations Part C: Mini-Talks	**50** 20 15 15	**40**
Section Two **Structure and Written Expression** Part A: Choose a correct word or phase Part B: Identify an incorrect word or phrase	**40 (60)** 15 25	**25 (35)**
Section Three **Vocabulary and Reading Comprehension** Part A: Synonyms Part B: Reading Comprehension	**60 (90)** 30 30	**45 (65)**
Section Four Essay	**1**	**30**
Total	**150 (200)** +Essay	**140 (170)**

The following chart is a guide to admission requirements at various educational institutions. It is only a guide. Admission requirements vary from institution to institution and from year to year.

Admissions Policy	Graduate Humanities	Graduate Science	Undergraduate	Technical School or 2–year College
Acceptable	550–600	500–600	500–600	450–600
Acceptable, with supplementary language training and reduced course load	500–550	450–500	400–500	400–450
Further English training required	Below 500	Below 450	Below 400	Below 400

❏ THE TOEFL: WHO TAKES IT?

Different language groups score differently on the TOEFL. You should recognize those areas that have statistically proved difficult for others in your language group and then focus on these areas during your preparation.

Language Groups	Listening Comprehension				Structure and Written Expression				Reading Comprehension and Vocabulary			
	45	50	55	60	45	50	55	60	45	50	55	60
Arabic												
Bengali												
Chinese												
Farsi												
French												
German												
Greek												
Hindi												
Ibo												
Indonesian												
Japanese												
Korean												
Malay												
Spanish												
Tagalog												
Thai												
Urdu												
Vietnamese												
Yoruba												

Source: Information is based on data from the TOEFL Test and Score Manual. 1987-88 Edition. Princeton, New Jersey: Educational Testing Service, p. 24.

❏ TOEFL INFORMATION

TOEFL BULLETIN

All candidates for the TOEFL will need the *TOEFL Bulletin of Information and Application Form*. This bulletin lists the TOEFL test centers around the world, provides information regarding the cost of the TOEFL, and includes an application form.

To receive a copy of the Bulletin outside the United States, contact the Cultural Affairs Officer of the local U.S. Information Service or an AMIDEAST or IIE regional office. You may also write directly to the TOEFL office:

TOEFL
P.O. Box 6151
Princeton, NJ 08541-6151
U.S.A.

Letter of Request

The letter you write may be similar to this:

Dear TOEFL Administrators:
Please send the latest edition of the *TOEFL Bulletin of Information and Application Form* to:
Print your name
Print your street address
Print your city, state/province
Print your postal code
Print your country
Sincerely,
Sign your name

TEST CENTERS

International, Special Center, and Institutional TOEFL

The International TOEFL and Special Center TOEFL are identical in question format, length and difficulty. New exams are given on each test date.

Test	Frequency/yr	Countries	Day
International TOEFL	6 times/yr	135	Saturday
Special Center TOEFL	6 times/yr	50	Friday

The Institutional TOEFL is used by local institutions and businesses to measure their students' language proficiency. The exam is scheduled at the convenience of the testing institution. Old exams are used for the Institutional TOEFL; consequently, the scores are not considered valid by university admissions officers.

REGISTRATION

International and Special Center TOEFL

You should complete the application in the *TOEFL Bulletin of Information and Application Form*. After the Educational Testing Service (ETS) receives your completed application and money, it will process a Confirmation Ticket for you. You will receive this Confirmation Ticket approximately one month before the test date.

Institutional TOEFL

Registration for the Institutional TOEFL is handled by the particular institutions administering these tests. You should contact them for more information.

SCORES

Current TOEFL Scores

On the day of the exam, you will be asked to list on your answer sheet four institutions, colleges, or universities that you wish to receive your scores. The institutions, colleges, or universities that you designate will receive the scores approximately one month after the test date. You also will receive your score approximately one month after you take the test.

If you listed fewer than four institutions, the remaining score reports will be sent to you. You may send them yourself to other colleges; however, the college may require an official score report received directly from ETS in Princeton.

Previous TOEFL Scores

The TOEFL scores are kept for only two years. If you took the test more than two years ago, you will have to take the TOEFL again to receive a new score.

If you took the test more than once, it is possible to have only your highest score sent to the institution or college. You will have to complete the *Request Form for Official Score Reports* and note the test date on which you scored higher.

GENERAL TEST–TAKING STRATEGIES

Before the Test
- Take a practice test in this book.
- Prepare your Personal Study Plan (PSP).
- Study the Targets indicated on your PSP.
- Read as much English as you can.
- Listen to as much English as you can.
- Relax the day before the exam.

On the Day of the Test
- Arrive on time.
- Bring only:
    (a) 3 or 4 No. 2 pencils with erasers
    (b) your Confirmation Ticket from ETS
    (c) your passport or photo identification
    (d) a watch
- Sit near the speakers.
- Make sure you are comfortable and can hear well.

During the Test
- Work rapidly but carefully.
- Do NOT read the directions.
- Read all choices carefully.
- Answer all the questions on your answer sheet. Do not leave blanks.
- Guess: if you have no idea which choice is correct, choose A (or your favorite letter). Leave no question unanswered.
- Keep your mind and eyes on your own test.
- Check to make sure that you have answered every question.
- Match the question number with the number on the answer sheet.
- Do the questions that seem easy first.
- Do NOT go back to previous sections.

GUESSING

There is no penalty for guessing. If you don't know an answer, make a guess. If you guess, it is better statistically always to guess using the same letter (always A, always B, always C, or always D-choose your favorite).

THE ANSWER SHEET

Your answer sheet is divided into columns with numbers followed by letters enclosed in ovals.

Sample Answer
Ⓐ Ⓑ Ⓒ Ⓓ

Each number stands for one question. There is only one answer per question. To mark an answer, completely fill in the corresponding oval. A soft lead (no. 2) pencil is best.
The day after Monday is

(A) Wednesday
(B) Sunday
(C) Tuesday
(D) Thursday

Sample Answer

DO NOT mark two answers.
Both will be counted wrong.

Sample Answer
● ● Ⓒ Ⓓ

DO NOT make any pencil marks elsewhere on the page. YOU MAY erase, but do it *completely.*

DO NOT DRAW arrows or make other marks. The test is scored by a machine that cannot read your messages. If it reads more than one answer per question, it marks the answers wrong.

PRACTICE TESTS

❏ HOW TO TAKE THE PRACTICE TESTS

The practice tests, when used with the Personal Study Plan, will give you an idea of your strengths and weaknesses in English. The results of the practice tests will guide you in studying for the TOEFL and will help you use your time wisely. Take the test as if you were taking the real TOEFL. Find a room where you will be undisturbed. Allow yourself three hours to take the exam.

The answer sheets are in the back of the book. Tear one out before you begin. Mark the answers on the answer sheet just as if you were taking the TOEFL.

You will need the tapes that accompany this book and a tape recorder to do the listening comprehension questions. If you do not have the tapes or a tape recorder, the tapescripts are in the back of the book. You can have someone read the tapescripts to you.

PERSONAL STUDY PLAN

When you finish a practice test, look at the Practice Test Explanatory Answer Key in the Appendix. The answers are coded according to the type of structure and listening questions being tested. The code refers you to a particular Target exercise to study. These Target exercises are listed on the Personal Study Plan: Listening Targets and the Personal Study Plan: Structure Targets. If you missed a question on a practice test, note the corresponding Target on your Personal Study Plan. For example, if the explanatory answer code says

23. (C) Word order: subject/verb

you should put a circle next to the Structure Target, Word order: subject/verb, in the appropriate practice test column.

PRACTICE TESTS

Structure	1	2	3	4
Word order: subject/verb	◯			

You should put a circle next to every Target you missed on the practice test. When you begin to study for the TOEFL, you should first study those Targets where you put a circle. This will make your study time more efficient. You can study these target areas in depth in the *Prentice Hall Regents Prep book for the TOEFL® Test: Four Practice Tests*.

❑ HOW TO SCORE THE PRACTICE TESTS

After you finish a practice test, you can tally your scores on each section. The chart below will help you determine your approximate total score. Add the three sections together and divide by 3 for your total score.

Number Correct	Score Section 1 *Listening Comprehension*	Score Section 2 *Structure and Written Expression*	Score Section 3 *Vocabulary and Reading Comprehension*
0	200	200	200
1	220	210	210
2	250	230	220
3	270	240	230
4	280	250	240
5	290	260	240
6	300	280	250
7	310	300	260
8	320	310	260
9	330	330	270
10	350	340	280
11	360	340	290
12	370	350	300
13	380	360	310
14	390	370	320

Number Correct	Score Section 1 Listening Comprehension	Score Section 2 Structure and Written Expression	Score Section 3 Vocabulary and Reading Comprehension
15	400	380	330
16	410	390	340
17	420	400	350
18	420	410	360
19	430	420	370
20	430	430	380
21	440	440	390
22	450	450	400
23	450	460	400
24	460	470	410
25	470	480	420
26	470	490	430
27	480	500	430
28	480	510	440
29	490	520	450
30	490	530	450
31	500	540	460
32	510	560	470
33	510	570	470
34	520	580	480
35	530	590	480
36	530	610	490
37	540	630	500
38	550	640	500
39	560	650	510
40	570	680	520
41	570	—	520
42	580	—	530
43	590	—	540
44	600	—	540
45	610	—	550
46	620	—	560
47	630	—	560

Number Correct	Score Section 1 *Listening Comprehension*	Score Section 2 *Structure and Written Expression*	Score Section 3 *Vocabulary and Reading Comprehension*
48	640	—	570
49	660	—	580
50	680	—	580
51	—	—	590
52	—	—	600
53	—	—	610
54	—	—	610
55	—	—	620
56	—	—	630
57	—	—	640
58	—	—	650
59	—	—	660
60	—	—	670

Practice Test	Score Section 1	Score Section 2	Score Section 3	Total Score	÷3	Approximate Score
1					÷3	
2					÷3	
3					÷3	
4					÷3	

PRACTICE TEST 1

SECTION 1

LISTENING COMPREHENSION

The questions in Section 1 of the test are on a recording.

In this section of the test, you will have an opportunity to demonstrate your ability to understand spoken English. There are three parts to this section, with special directions for each part.

Part A

Directions: For each question in Part A, you will hear a short sentence. Each sentence will be spoken just one time. The sentence you hear will not be written out for you. Therefore, you must listen carefully to understand what the speaker says.

After you hear a sentence, read the four choices in your test book, marked (A), (B), (C), and (D), and decide which *one* is closest in meaning to the sentence you heard. Then, on your answer sheet, find the number of the question and fill in the space that matches the letter of the answer you have chosen. Fill in the space so that the letter inside the oval cannot be seen.

Example I   **Sample Answer**
  You will hear: *Mary swam out to the island with her*   Ⓐ Ⓑ ● Ⓓ
                               friends.
  You will read: (A) Mary outswam the others.
                      (B) Mary ought to swim with them.
                      (C) Mary and her friends swam to the island.
                      (D) Mary's friends owned the island.

The speaker said, "Mary swam out to the island with her friends." Sentence (C), "Mary and her friends swam to the island," is closest in meaning to the sentence you heard. Therefore, you should choose answer (C).

Example II   **Sample Answer**
  You will hear: *Would you mind helping me with this load of*   Ⓐ ● Ⓒ Ⓓ
                               books?
  You will read: (A) Please remind me to read this book.
                      (B) Could you help me carry these books?
                      (C) I don't mind if you help me.
                      (D) Do you have a heavy course load?

The speaker said, "Would you mind helping me with this load of books?" Sentence (B), "Could you help me carry these books?" is closest in meaning to the sentence you heard. Therefore, you should choose answer (B).

GO ON TO THE NEXT PAGE

1. (A) Joan will take a plane.
    (B) Joan's father will drive.
    (C) Joan and I will come by car.
    (D) Joan likes to drive.

2. (A) Walking is the best exercise.
    (B) Walking is not as good an
         exercise as swimming.
    (C) Swimming is good for you.
    (D) Swimming and walking are both
         good exercises.

3. (A) Don't stand in the sun.
    (B) Put your hands in the air now.
    (C) Let me know if you want an
         explanation.
    (D) You never understand anything.

4. (A) It may rain this morning.
    (B) The local weather is always the
         same.
    (C) The news comes before the
         weather report.
    (D) I never follow the weather
         report.

5. (A) Someone is following Margaret.
    (B) Margaret gives easy directions.
    (C) Only Margaret can follow
         directions.
    (D) People should follow Margaret.

6. (A) The two of us went to the
         movies.
    (B) Mary saw one movie after the
         other.
    (C) Both movies started at noon.
    (D) Mary wanted to go to the movies
         on Tuesday.

7. (A) Mark got off first.
    (B) Mark took the last bus.
    (C) Everyone got off before Mark.
    (D) Mark missed the last bus.

8. (A) You shouldn't do so much
         work.
    (B) There is too much work for
         you.
    (C) You usually don't do so much.
    (D) There's not enough work to do.

9. (A) Are you free to have lunch
         together soon?
    (B) Why don't you eat lunch every
         day?
    (C) Why do we always have lunch
         at the same place?
    (D) Are we having lunch today?

10. (A) Our friends moved to the city
         recently.
    (B) We moved to be closer to our
         friends.
    (C) We developed new friendships
         when we moved.
    (D) We moved to the city with our
         friends.

11. (A) We did not wait inside.
    (B) If it were warmer, I'd stay
         outside.
    (C) It was too hot to wait outside.
    (D) We waited for warmer
         weather.

GO ON TO THE NEXT PAGE

12. (A) Buy me some stamps if you go near the post office.
    (B) You bought some stamps at the post office.
    (C) I'll buy some stamps at the post office.
    (D) I passed the post office this morning.

13. (A) I won't be late tomorrow.
    (B) I won't be on time tomorrow.
    (C) I won't eat until tomorrow.
    (D) I'm sorry I can't be there tomorrow.

14. (A) The gym is above the Athletic Office.
    (B) Jim signed up in the locker room.
    (C) To get to the Athletic Office, you have to go upstairs.
    (D) You must apply for a locker in the Athletic Office.

15. (A) Are you learning to play any music?
    (B) Do you like classical music better than rock?
    (C) Do you listen to rock music?
    (D) Are you taking a music class this semester?

16. (A) The afternoon mail has already come.
    (B) The letter will arrive on Monday if it's mailed today.
    (C) They should receive your letters this afternoon.
    (D) You shouldn't mail the letter until next Monday.

17. (A) The library closes at 6:00 this evening and is not open tomorrow.
    (B) The library is closed tonight.
    (C) Tomorrow the library closes at 6:00.
    (D) The library closes at 6:00 tonight and tomorrow.

18. (A) The room is very bright.
    (B) Please turn on another lamp.
    (C) The light is better in the other room.
    (D) The other light is much better.

19. (A) The class started before I arrived.
    (B) I didn't do the experiment.
    (C) It was difficult to follow the directions.
    (D) Don't start the experiment without reading the directions.

20. (A) I always read on the weekends.
    (B) I finished the book last week.
    (C) I have to read all of the book by Saturday.
    (D) I'll make a bookcase this weekend.

GO ON TO THE NEXT PAGE

Part B

Directions: In Part B you will hear short conversations between two speakers. At the end of each conversation, a third person will ask a question about what was said. You will hear each conversation and question about it just one time. The sentence you hear will not be written out for you. Therefore, you must listen carefully to understand what the speaker says. After you hear a conversation and the question about it, read the four possible answers in your test book and decide which one is the best answer to the question you heard. Then, on your answer sheet, find the number of the question and fill in the space that matches the letter of the answer you have chosen.

Example   **Sample Answer**
                                                                          ● Ⓑ Ⓒ Ⓓ

You will hear:
    (first man) *Professor Smith is going to retire soon. What kind of gift shall we give her?*
    (woman) *I think she'd like to have a photograph of our class.*
    (second man) *What does the woman think the class should do?*
You will read: (A) Present Professor Smith with a picture.
                 (B) Photograph Professor Smith.
                 (C) Put glass over the photograph.
                 (D) Replace the broken headlight.

From the conversation you learn that the woman thinks Professor Smith would like a photograph of the class. The best answer to the question "What does the woman think the class should do?" is (A), "Present Professor Smith with a picture." Therefore, you should choose answer (A).

21. (A) At a police station.
    (B) At a military post.
    (C) At an employment agency.
    (D) At a bank.

22. (A) She missed her appointment.
    (B) She's sick.
    (C) She's a busy doctor.
    (D) She's cold.

23. (A) At a movie theater.
    (B) At a bus stop.
    (C) In a train station.
    (D) On a football field.

24. (A) Go shopping.
    (B) Brew tea.
    (C) Make a cake.
    (D) Serve coffee.

25. (A) Once a week.
    (B) Twice a week.
    (C) Three times a week.
    (D) Every day.

26. (A) Phone later.
    (B) Try harder.
    (C) Get busy.
    (D) Look up the number again.

GO ON TO THE NEXT PAGE ▶

27. (A) Go to a movie.
    (B) Go home.
    (C) Eat dinner.
    (D) Meet their friends.

28. (A) He can't eat in the restaurant.
    (B) He can't smoke.
    (C) He's in the wrong restaurant.
    (D) He doesn't like people who smoke.

29. (A) He's afraid of flying.
    (B) He's nervous.
    (C) He wants more coffee.
    (D) He lost his watch.

30. (A) The man doesn't know how to read.
    (B) He can't see without his glasses.
    (C) He lost his vision.
    (D) He forgot his car.

31. (A) Start school.
    (B) Park her car.
    (C) Go to the park.
    (D) Open an office.

32. (A) Stop working.
    (B) Buy new tires.
    (C) Fix the door.
    (D) Take a walk.

33. (A) At a supermarket.
    (B) At a power plant.
    (C) At a gas station.
    (D) At a tennis match.

34. (A) She can't come to lunch tomorrow.
    (B) She has to take a train.
    (C) She doesn't join clubs.
    (D) She'd like to meet his friend.

35. (A) In a restaurant.
    (B) At a library.
    (C) At a hotel.
    (D) In a classroom.

GO ON TO THE NEXT PAGE

Part C

Directions: In this part of the test, you will hear short talks and conversations. After each of them, you will be asked some questions. You will hear the talks and conversations just one time. They will not be written out for you. Therefore, you must listen carefully in order to understand what the speaker says.

After you hear a question, read the four possible answers in your test book and decide which one is the best answer to the question you heard. Then, on your answer sheet, find the number of the question and fill in the space that matches the letter of the answer you have chosen.

Answer all questions on the basis of what is *stated* or *implied* in the talk or conversation.

Listen to this sample talk.
  You will hear:
    (first man) *Balloons have been used for about a hundred years. There are two kinds of sport balloons, gas and hot air. Hot-air balloons are safer than gas balloons, which may catch fire. Hot-air balloons are preferred by most balloonists in the United States because of their safety. They are also cheaper and easier to manage than gas balloons. Despite the ease of operating a balloon, pilots must watch the weather carefully. Sport balloon flights are best early in the morning or late in the afternoon, when the wind is light.*

Now look at the following example.   **Sample Answer**
  You will hear: Ⓐ ● Ⓒ Ⓓ
    (second man) *Why are gas balloons considered dangerous?*
    You will read: (A) They are impossible to guide.
                        (B) They may go up in flames.
                        (C) They tend to leak gas.
                        (D) They are cheaply made.
  The best answer to the question "Why are gas balloons considered dangerous?" is (B), "They may go up in flames." Therefore, you should choose answer (B).

GO ON TO THE NEXT PAGE

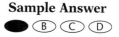

Now look at the next example.
  You will hear: **Sample Answer**
    (second man) *According to the speaker, what must balloon*   ● Ⓑ Ⓒ Ⓓ
                      pilots be careful to do?
  You will read: (A) Watch for changes in weather.
                      (B) Watch their altitude.
                      (C) Check for weak spots in their balloons.
                      (D) Test the strength of the ropes.
    The best answer to the question "According to the speaker, what must balloon
pilots be careful to do?" is (A), "Watch for changes in weather." Therefore, you
should choose answer (A).

36. (A) Dreams.
     (B) Scientific investigations.
     (C) Happiness.
     (D) Crowds.

37. (A) Only since this year.
     (B) At the turn of the century.
     (C) Since a long time ago.
     (D) Within the last ten years.

38. (A) One.
     (B) Four.
     (C) Five.
     (D) Six.

39. (A) Relaxed.
     (B) Resting.
     (C) Rapid.
     (D) Romantic.

40. (A) Dreams.
     (B) Wakefulness.
     (C) Friendship.
     (D) Loneliness.

41. (A) Frustration.
     (B) Happiness.
     (C) Anger.
     (D) Restfulness.

42. (A) Whether or not the girl will
          become deaf.
     (B) How loudly her daughter plays
          the music.
     (C) That high noise levels are
          harmful to them.
     (D) That she's talking too loud.

43. (A) One.
     (B) Two.
     (C) One hundred.
     (D) One hundred thirty.

44. (A) People in their 20s.
     (B) Senior citizens.
     (C) Airline pilots.
     (D) Music librarians.

GO ON TO THE NEXT PAGE

45. (A) 95.
    (B) 130.
    (C) 150.
    (D) 200.

46. (A) The first week of class.
    (B) The end of the semester.
    (C) During the first exam.
    (D) The middle of the term.

47. (A) Home economics.
    (B) Anthropology.
    (C) Social welfare.
    (D) Archaeology.

48. (A) They are thrifty.
    (B) They are wasteful.
    (C) They are quality-oriented.
    (D) They are usually poor.

49. (A) Choice cuts of meat.
    (B) Educational toys.
    (C) Low-quality produce.
    (D) Expensive kitchen materials.

50. (A) To gather information from it.
    (B) To clean up their neighborhoods.
    (C) To become better consumers.
    (D) To avoid poor eating habits.

THIS IS THE END OF THE LISTENING COMPREHENSION SECTION OF THE TEST

THE NEXT PART OF THE TEST IS SECTION 2. TURN TO THE DIRECTIONS FOR SECTION 2 IN YOUR TEST BOOK. READ THEM, AND BEGIN WORK. DO NOT READ OR WORK ON ANY OTHER SECTION OF THE TEST.

STOP   STOP   STOP   **STOP**   STOP   STOP   STOP

SECTION 2
STRUCTURE AND WRITTEN EXPRESSION

Time: 25 minutes

This section tests your ability to recognize language that is appropriate for standard written English. There are two types of questions in this section, with special directions for each type.

Directions: Questions 1–15 are incomplete sentences. Beneath each sentence, you will see four words or phrases, marked (A), (B), (C), and (D). Choose the *one* word or phrase that best completes the sentence. Then, on your answer sheet, find the number of the question and fill in the space that corresponds to the letter of the answer you have chosen. Fill in the space so that the letter inside the oval cannot be seen.

Example I   **Sample Answer**

Vegetables are an excellent source _____ vitamins.
(A) of
(B) has
(C) where
(D) that
The sentence should read, "Vegetables are an excellent source of vitamins." Therefore, you should choose answer (A).

Example II   **Sample Answer**

_____ in history when remarkable progress was made within a relatively short span of time.
(A) Periods
(B) Throughout periods
(C) There have been periods
(D) Periods have been
The sentence should read, "There have been periods in history when remarkable progress was made within a relatively short span of time." Therefore, you should choose answer (C).

Now begin work on the questions.

GO ON TO THE NEXT PAGE

Structure and Written Expression **13**

1. _____, the world's economic leaders have been the dominant political and military powers.
   (A) Traditional
   (B) Traditionally
   (C) The tradition
   (D) A tradition

2. Corporations of the future will be _____ those that flourished in recent years.
   (A) differ from
   (B) different from
   (C) different
   (D) difference

3. Occupations in _____ current participants have the most education are projected to have the most rapid growth rate.
   (A) that
   (B) which
   (C) who
   (D) these

4. Because counterfeit products are often of substandard quality, _____ a potential for safety risks.
   (A) there are
   (B) it is
   (C) they are
   (D) there is

5. The worldwide warming of _____ threatens to raise the earth's average temperature by 1.5–4.5 degrees Celsius by the year 2050.
   (A) atmosphere
   (B) an atmosphere
   (C) the atmosphere
   (D) any atmosphere

6. Over a billion people live in countries that are already _____ firewood shortages.
   (A) experienced
   (B) experiencing
   (C) experience
   (D) have experienced

7. As society grows increasingly dependent on technology, computer skills are not just desirable, _____ essential.
   (A) and
   (B) but
   (C) for
   (D) not

8. At the turn of the century, scientists wondered whether the atoms of chemical elements were _____ of smaller particles.
   (A) been composed
   (B) composing
   (C) to compose
   (D) composed

9. The Census Bureau for years used the completion of the fourth grade as _____ standard of literacy.
   (A) its
   (B) it's
   (C) their
   (D) there is

GO ON TO THE NEXT PAGE ▶

10. For every ton of grain _____,
    American farmers were losing six
    tons of their top soil.
    (A) they produced
    (B) which produced
    (C) that were producing
    (D) they are producing

11. From about 1910–1930, most
    physicists believed _____ atomic
    energy would be of no practical
    value.
    (A) in
    (B) that
    (C) for
    (D) which

12. Over 2,100 valley residents and
    visitors lost _____ lives in the
    Johnstown Flood.
    (A) their
    (B) they're
    (C) there
    (D) themselves

13. If our future is to be
    environmentally and _____
    sustainable, many adjustments will
    have to be made.
    (A) economic
    (B) economy
    (C) economically
    (D) economical

14. The first zoological garden in the
    United States _____ in
    Philadelphia in 1874.
    (A) was establishing
    (B) being established
    (C) establishing
    (D) was established

15. Jet lag is more pronounced in older
    adults _____ motion sickness is a
    problem for the young.
    (A) for
    (B) or
    (C) by
    (D) while

GO ON TO THE NEXT PAGE

Structure and Written Expression **15**

Directions: In questions 16–40, each sentence has four underlined words or phrases. The four underlined parts of the sentence are marked (A), (B), (C), and (D). Identify the *one* underlined word or phrase that must be changed in order for the sentence to be correct. Then, on your answer sheet, find the number of the question and fill in the space that corresponds to the letter of the answer you have chosen.

Example I   **Sample Answer**
                                                               Ⓐ Ⓑ ● Ⓓ

 A ray of light passing <u>through</u> <u>the center</u> of a thin lens <u>keep</u> its original <u>direction</u>.
       A   **B**   **C**   **D**

 The sentence should read, "A ray of light passing through the center of a thin lens keeps its original direction." Therefore, you should choose answer (C).

Example II   **Sample Answer**
                                                               Ⓐ Ⓑ Ⓒ ●

 The mandolin, a musical <u>instrument</u> <u>that has</u> strings, was probably copied <u>from</u>
           A   **B**   **C**

the lute, a <u>many</u> older instrument.
    D

 The sentence should read, "The mandolin, a musical instrument that has strings, was probably copied from the lute, a much older instrument." Therefore, you should choose answer (D).

 Now begin work on the questions.

16. <u>A</u> writer of biographies <u>are</u> heavily influenced <u>by</u> the <u>dominant</u> literary theory.
   A   **B**   **C**   **D**

17. Birds have a <u>relatively</u> large brain, keen sight, and acute <u>hearing</u>, but <u>they little</u>
        A   **B**   **C**

<u>sense of</u> smell.
  D

GO ON TO THE NEXT PAGE

18. Bonds, which were <u>sold</u> by the U.S. government <u>to finance</u> both world wars,
                 A   **B**

    <u>and</u> <u>are</u> still an important money-<u>raising</u> device.
     C   **D**

19. <u>Unlikely</u> <u>sound</u>, light <u>can travel</u> <u>through</u> a vacuum.
     A   **B**   **C**   **D**

20. Vegetarians who <u>drinking</u> <u>no</u> alcohol and <u>do</u> not smoke live <u>longer than</u> the
                   A   **B**   **C**   **D**

    general population.

21. <u>Consumer</u> protection groups <u>like</u> the Consumer Guardian <u>checks</u> the safety and
     A   **B**   **C**

    <u>reliability</u> of products and services.
     D

22. Citizens can <u>become affiliated</u> with a political party <u>by check</u> the appropriate
               A   **B**

    box when <u>they</u> register <u>to vote</u>.
          C   **D**

23. <u>The</u> psychologist B.F. Skinner <u>is know</u> for <u>his</u> studies of conditions that <u>affect</u>
   A   **B**   **C**   **D**

    the learning of behavior.

24. <u>Scientists have</u> <u>proof</u> that groups of songbirds <u>have</u> <u>its</u> own distinct dialects.
        A   **B**   **C** **D**

25. The growing number of old people in America means <u>there is</u> a <u>need growing</u>
                                            A   **B**

    for <u>service</u> workers <u>in</u> the health care field.
        C   **D**

26. Conditions <u>like</u> being too fat or <u>too thinner</u> are both <u>associated with</u>
            A   **B**   **C**

    <u>increased health</u> risks.
        D

GO ON TO THE NEXT PAGE

27. Socialist governments provide many social welfare programs such as healthy
     A   B   C

     care and aid to the poor.
                    D

28. Cells can exist independently of other cells and which are capable of
     A   B   C

     reproducing themselves.
                 D

29. Leaves that seemingly turn yellow or orange in autumn has actually contained
            A   B   C

     that color throughout the summer.
                           D

30. Most small mammals live only two or three years, while an elephant may life
                                      A   B   C

     for as long as sixty years.
     D

31. Recent experiments conducted on laboratory animals have shown that exposing
                        A   have shown   C
                                                         B

     to ozone gas in great quantities may cause cancer.
                  D

32. When hot and cold water they are mixed together, the hot water will give up
                        A   B   C

     heat to the cold water.
             D

33. The Amazon River flows largely through the sparsely inhabited jungles of Brazil
                      A   B

     on their way to the Atlantic Ocean.
        C   D

34. Consumers who spend more money on automobiles than on furniture and
               A   B   C

     household equipment.
     D

GO ON TO THE NEXT PAGE ▶

18 Practice Test 1

35. The first <u>elevator electric</u> was <u>installed</u> in New York City <u>in</u> 1889.
    A   **B**   **C**   **D**

36. Honey, a <u>food found</u> in the tombs of ancient Egypt, <u>is the</u> only food <u>that not</u>
           A   **B**   **C**

    <u>spoil</u>.
    D

37. The <u>federal</u> government can increase taxes <u>or decrease</u> spending <u>to reducing</u>
      A   **B**   **C**

    the size of <u>its</u> debt.
           D

38. <u>On a hot</u> day, the <u>land heats up</u> <u>faster</u> than <u>ocean</u>.
    A   **B**   **C**   **D**

39. <u>Contrarily</u> to what we would <u>expect</u>, scientists <u>measure</u> distance, not time,
    A   **B**   **C**

    by using "light years."
    D

40. The Mississippi River is <u>the long</u> river <u>in the United States</u>, and <u>is the</u> nation's
                        A   **B**   **C**

    <u>most important</u> inland waterway.
    D

THIS IS THE END OF SECTION 2

IF YOU FINISH BEFORE TIME IS CALLED, CHECK YOUR WORK
ON SECTION 2 ONLY.
DO NOT READ OR WORK ON ANY OTHER SECTION OF THE TEST.
THE SUPERVISOR WILL TELL YOU WHEN TO BEGIN WORK
ON SECTION 3.

SECTION 3
VOCABULARY AND READING COMPREHENSION

Time: 45 minutes

This section tests your comprehension of standard written English. There are two types of questions in this section, with special directions for each type.

Directions: In questions 1–30, each sentence has an underlined word or phrase. Below each sentence are four other words or phrases, marked (A), (B), (C), and (D). You are to choose the *one* word or phrase that *best keeps the meaning* of the original sentence if it is substituted for the underlined word or phrase. Then, on your answer sheet, find the number of the question and fill in the space that matches the letter you have chosen. Fill in the space so that the letter inside the oval cannot be seen.

Example   **Sample Answer**

Passenger ships and <u>aircraft</u> are often equipped with ship-to-shore or air-to-land radio telephones.   Ⓐ Ⓑ ⬤ Ⓓ

(A) highways
(B) railroads
(C) planes
(D) sailboats

The best answer is (C), because "Passenger ships and planes are often equipped with ship-to-shore or air-to-land radio telephones" is closest in meaning to the original sentence. Therefore, you should choose answer (C).

Now begin work on the questions.

1. Countries export their <u>excess</u> resources and products.
   (A) valuable
   (B) inferior
   (C) surplus
   (D) expensive

2. No one may copy an invention without the <u>permission</u> of the patent holder.
   (A) signature
   (B) consent
   (C) intervention
   (D) persistence

GO ON TO THE NEXT PAGE

3. Religious practices are often dependent on a culture's <u>environment</u>.
   (A) history
   (B) government
   (C) beliefs
   (D) surroundings

4. When the United States entered World War I, some people thought women should <u>cease</u> their attempts to get the vote.
   (A) stop
   (B) prolong
   (C) increase
   (D) postpone

5. Platinum is an unusually <u>dense</u> metal, twice as heavy as silver and one-third heavier than gold.
   (A) expensive
   (B) concentrated
   (C) dark
   (D) common

6. Throughout history, <u>settlements</u> have grown where one kind of transportation ended and another began.
   (A) stations
   (B) communities
   (C) tenements
   (D) crops

7. Satellite photos help a cartographer draw <u>accurate</u> maps.
   (A) colorful
   (B) circular
   (C) weather
   (D) precise

8. The first <u>permanent</u> English colony in North America was Jamestown, Virginia
   (A) period
   (B) enduring
   (C) successful
   (D) established

9. Stings of bees, wasps, and ants can have life-threatening, even <u>fatal</u> results in minutes.
   (A) inconvenient
   (B) annoying
   (C) deadly
   (D) unbelievable

10. Social indicators <u>depict</u> the standard of living more accurately than do economic statistics.
    (A) predict
    (B) illustrate
    (C) determine
    (D) stimulate

11. Concern for protecting a country's workers <u>motivates</u> popular support for trade tariffs.
    (A) determines
    (B) hastens
    (C) prevents
    (D) encourages

12. One <u>barrier</u> to world peace is the nuclear arms buildup.
    (A) obstacle
    (B) threat
    (C) end
    (D) contribution

GO ON TO THE NEXT PAGE

13. Florence Nightingale, who <u>reformed</u> the British Army, was the founder of modern nursing.
    (A) led
    (B) improved
    (C) established
    (D) challenged

14. Irrigation is required to grow crops in <u>arid</u> areas.
    (A) urban
    (B) fertile
    (C) dry
    (D) mountainous

15. Scientific experiments with animal subjects that <u>proliferated</u> in the 1950s are on the decline.
    (A) increased
    (B) started
    (C) disappeared
    (D) improved

16. The American sculptor Isamu Noguchi is a <u>celebrated</u> designer of furniture and costumes.
    (A) fanciful
    (B) celibate
    (C) famous
    (D) creative

17. The <u>phenomenal</u> growth of the suburbs has increased the demand for better roads.
    (A) recent
    (B) extraordinary
    (C) predicted
    (D) gradual

18. Differences in climate mean differences in temperature, <u>precipitation</u>, and the length of the growing season.
    (A) rainfall
    (B) altitude
    (C) topography
    (D) winds

19. By 1900, the United States had <u>shifted</u> from being a country of farmers to a country of factory workers.
    (A) drifted
    (B) changed
    (C) improved
    (D) geared itself

20. The Dawes Act of 1887 encouraged Native Americans to become farmers and give up their tribal <u>practices</u>.
    (A) religions
    (B) leaders
    (C) lands
    (D) customs

21. <u>Infectious</u> diseases have increased as a major cause of death.
    (A) Adolescent
    (B) Insidious
    (C) Fatal
    (D) Contagious

GO ON TO THE NEXT PAGE

22. Technology has provided a way to <u>recycle</u> water but not purify it.
    (A) pump
    (B) freeze
    (C) reuse
    (D) deliver

23. <u>Compulsory</u> education was established to improve the lot of the working classes.
    (A) Vocational
    (B) Secondary
    (C) Obligatory
    (D) Universal

24. When World War I broke out in Europe in 1914, the United States remained <u>neutral</u> at first.
    (A) nonaligned
    (B) belligerent
    (C) prepared
    (D) isolated

25. Most parents are unaware of how <u>ineffectively</u> they react when their children misbehave.
    (A) naturally
    (B) futilely
    (C) emotionally
    (D) reasonably

26. After World War II, the United States and Russia <u>emerged as</u> world powers.
    (A) remained
    (B) became
    (C) competed as
    (D) functioned as

27. Iceland is a <u>remote</u>, romantic island in the Atlantic Ocean.
    (A) changeable
    (B) lovely
    (C) turbulent
    (D) distant

28. The Civil Rights Act of 1964 <u>prohibited</u> discrimination in voting.
    (A) encouraged
    (B) forbade
    (C) proposed
    (D) reduced

29. The *Iliad* and the *Odyssey* are both <u>popularly</u> attributed to Homer.
    (A) infamously
    (B) knowingly
    (C) usually
    (D) generously

30. <u>Instructive</u> pictures are taken of the planet earth from satellites hovering above.
    (A) Informative
    (B) Detailed
    (C) Delayed
    (D) Frequent

GO ON TO THE NEXT PAGE

Directions: In the rest of this section you will read several passages. Each one is followed by several questions about it. For questions 31–60, you are to choose the *one* best answer, (A), (B), (C), or (D), to each question. Then, on your answer sheet, find the number of the question and fill in the space that matches the letter of the answer you have chosen.

Answer all questions following a passage on the basis of what is *stated* or *implied* in the reading passage.

Example passage and questions

The rattles with which a rattlesnake warns of its presence are formed by loosely interlocking hollow rings of hard skin, which make a buzzing sound when its tail is shaken. As a baby, the snake begins to form its rattles from the button at the very tip of its tail. Thereafter, each time it sheds its skin, a new ring is formed. Popular belief holds that a snake's age can be told by counting the rings, but this idea is fallacious. In fact, a snake may lose its old skin as often as four times a year. Also, rattles tend to wear or break off with time.

Example

A rattlesnake's rattles are made of
(A) skin
(B) bone
(C) wood
(D) muscle

Sample Answer

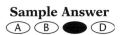

According to the passage, a rattlesnake's rattles are made of rings of hard skin. Therefore, you should choose answer (A).

Example

How often does a rattlesnake shed its skin?
(A) Once every four years
(B) Once every four months
(C) Up to four times every year
(D) Four times more often than other snakes

Sample Answer

The passage states that "a snake may lose its old skin as often as four times a year." Therefore, you should choose answer (C).

Now begin work on the questions.

GO ON TO THE NEXT PAGE

Questions 31–36

The sun's radiation striking the earth supplies the energy to heat the ocean surface and to warm the lower atmosphere. Energy from the sun is filtered as it passes through the atmosphere and is filtered again in surface ocean waters. Within the first 10 centimeters of even pure water, virtually all the infrared portion of the light spectrum is absorbed and changed into heat. Within the first meter of seawater, about 60 percent of the entering radiation is absorbed, and about 80 percent is absorbed in the first 10 meters. Only about 1 percent remains at 140 meters in the clearest subtropical ocean waters.

In coastal waters, abundant marine organisms, suspended sediment particles, and dissolved organic substances absorb light at even shallower depths. Near Cape Cod, Massachusetts, for instance, only 1 percent of the surface light commonly penetrates to 16 meters. In such waters the maximum transparency shifts from the bluish region typical of clear oceanic waters to longer wavelengths. In turbid coastal waters, absorption of all light takes place within a few centimeters of the water surface.

Far from the coast, ocean water often has a deep luminous blue color quite unlike the greenish or brownish colors common to coastal waters. The deep blue color indicates an absence of particles, i.e., clean water. In these areas, the color of the water is thought to result from a scattering of light rays within the water. A similar type of scattering is responsible for the blue color of the clean atmosphere.

31. How is the ocean surface heated?
    (A) By the radiation hitting the earth
    (B) By warming the atmosphere
    (C) By warm water rising to the surface
    (D) By the movement of the ocean's waters

32. The sun's energy is first filtered by
    (A) the ocean
    (B) the atmosphere
    (C) suspended sediment
    (D) tropical currents

33. The greatest percentage of radiation entering seawater is absorbed within the first
    (A) meter
    (B) 10 meters
    (C) 16 meters
    (D) 140 meters

34. Where are the clearest waters likely to be found?
    (A) In coastal waters
    (B) In subtropical areas
    (C) Around Cape Cod
    (D) Around marine organisms

GO ON TO THE NEXT PAGE

35. In which of the following would you most likely find the color deep blue?
    (A) In shallow waters
    (B) In clean waters
    (C) In turbid waters
    (D) In coastal harbors

36. What is the cause of the deep blue color of the ocean?
    (A) Scattering of light rays
    (B) Abundant marine organisms
    (C) Absorption of light
    (D) Proliferation of particles

Questions 37–43

Design, although we can usually recognize it, is, like art, hard to define. It has been described as intention—the alternative to chance—which indicates that anything that is designed is thought about and conclusions are reached that result in a particular arrangement of the elements and a specific relationship of the parts. The design of buildings involves consideration of construction materials, setting, function, etc.

There is a further element in design, which is expressed by Professor Pevsner's distinction between building and architecture. "A bicycle shed is a building; Lincoln Cathedral is a piece of architecture." Nearly everything that encloses space on a scale sufficient for human beings to move in is a building; the term architecture applies only to a building designed with a view to aesthetic appeal.

Pevsner suggests that in architecture the design also must incorporate "aesthetic appeal." This certainly is the study of beauty and ugliness, the philosophy of taste. From this we may conclude that amid all his practical decisions, the architect must also consider the beauty or ugliness of his structure. Simply taking beauty into consideration will result in architecture, but whether it is good or bad architecture will depend on the architect's sensitivity, his "taste" and as the reader will now suppose, his success or failure will lie in the individual judgment of the observer.

The same considerations, of course, also apply to the other visual arts. Aesthetics, notions of beauty and ugliness, truth and falsehood, the pseudo and the real, are the constant preoccupations of aestheticians and all other students of the arts. Value judgments are what appreciation and understanding are all about.

GO ON TO THE NEXT PAGE

37. The author of the passage believes that design, like art, is
    (A) easily recognizable, but difficult to define
    (B) very easy to define
    (C) hard to recognize
    (D) unintentional

38. Which of the following was NOT included in the list of design considerations?
    (A) Equipment
    (B) Cost
    (C) Location
    (D) Purpose

39. Professor Pevsner makes a distinction between architecture and
    (A) aesthetic appeal
    (B) art
    (C) building
    (D) function

40. In the second paragraph, how does the author define architecture?
    (A) As a tasteful building
    (B) As a bicycle shed
    (C) As a scaled space
    (D) As moveable

41. What determines whether the architect was successful?
    (A) The opinion of the observers
    (B) The functionality of the building
    (C) The endurance of the structure
    (D) The architect's sensitivity

42. Which of the following characteristics would the author think most important?
    (A) Practicality
    (B) Consistency
    (C) Sensitivity
    (D) Honesty

43. What do aestheticians share with other students of the arts?
    (A) Longing for success
    (B) Disregard for functionality
    (C) Considerations of aesthetic appeal
    (D) Observant critics

GO ON TO THE NEXT PAGE

Questions 44–48

Value judgments cannot be made in science in the way that such judgments are made in philosophy, religion, and the arts, and indeed in our daily lives. Whether or not something is good or beautiful or right in a moral sense, for example, cannot be determined by scientific methods. Such judgments, even though they may be supported by a broad consensus, are not subject to scientific testing.

At one time, the sciences, like the arts, were pursued for their own sake. They were pursued for pleasure and satisfaction of the insatiable curiosity with which we are both cursed and blessed. In the twentieth century, however, the sciences have spawned a host of giant technological achievements—the hydrogen bomb, the polio vaccine, pesticides, indestructible plastics, nuclear energy plants, perhaps even ways to manipulate our genetic heritage—but have not given us any clues about how to use them wisely. Moreover, science, as a result of these very achievements, appears enormously powerful. It is thus little wonder that there are many people who are angry at science, as one would be angry at an omnipotent authority who apparently has the power to grant one's wishes but who refuses to do so.

The reason that science cannot and does not solve the problems we want it to is inherent in its nature. Most of the problems we now confront can be solved only by value judgments. For example, science gave us nuclear power and can give us predictions as to the extent of the biological damage that might result from accidents that allowed varying levels of radioactivity to escape into the environment. Yet it cannot help us, as citizens, in weighing the risk of damage from conceivable accidents against our energy needs. It can give us data to weigh our judgments on, but it cannot make those judgments for us.

44. Why does the author feel that science and the arts were similar?
    (A) Both were intensely sought after
    (B) Both had enormous power
    (C) Both made people angry
    (D) Both helped solve many problems

45. Which of the following is the best title for the passage?
    (A) Technological Achievements of the Twentieth Century
    (B) Science versus Art
    (C) Art for Art's Sake
    (D) Scientific Investigation and Value Judgments

46. With which of the following statements would the author of the passage LEAST agree?
    (A) Science creates more problems than it solves.
    (B) Science is enormously powerful.
    (C) Science can measure right and wrong.
    (D) Science can make predictions about nuclear damage.

GO ON TO THE NEXT PAGE

47. What is the author's attitude toward science?
    (A) Objective
    (B) Pessimistic
    (C) Awed
    (D) Disgusted

48. Which of the following would NOT be a subject of scientific inquiry?
    (A) Manipulating genetic heritage
    (B) Being right in a moral sense
    (C) Measuring levels of radioactivity
    (D) Developing indestructible plastics

Questions 49–52

Since art forgery is a very big business, enormous sums of money are involved, and the successful passing off of a fake will be very rewarding. In consequence, a great deal of ingenuity is devoted to establishing the authenticity of a work of art. In many instances its provenance (place of origin) and its successive owners, in the case
5 of an historical work, are known, and its authenticity, if not its quality, is unchallengeable. Many works in public galleries and private collections are of this order.

Frequently, however, there are gaps in the histories of many works—sometimes covering many centuries. In these circumstances the internal evidence in the work
10 itself—its material, its finish, its condition, its similarity to other works by the same artist from the same period—has to be considered and specialist expertise consulted.

49. In line 2, the word *fake* refers to which of the following?
    (A) Counterfeit money
    (B) A phony artist
    (C) A piece of art
    (D) Big collectors

50. The provenance of a work of art refers to
    (A) how well it's crafted
    (B) how beautiful it is
    (C) its success
    (D) where it's from

51. To prove the authenticity of a work of art whose past is only partly known, one usually
    (A) considers the internal evidence
    (B) considers the external evidence
    (C) consults successive owners
    (D) consults public galleries and private collections

52. Which of the following is the best title for the passage?
    (A) How to Make Enormous Sums of Money from Art
    (B) How to Establish the Authenticity of a Work of Art
    (C) The Business of Forging Art
    (D) Ordering Art from Public Galleries

GO ON TO THE NEXT PAGE

Questions 53–56

The Food and Drug Administration (FDA) was created by Congress in 1906, primarily to address unsanitary conditions in the nation's food industries and to control the sale of dangerous and ineffective medicines. Its legislation essentially required the correct labeling of food and drugs and the inspection and certification of food industries by this agency in the U.S. Department of Agriculture. A "pure food" certification from the federal government protected domestic markets and export sales to Europe. Government certification remains a critical factor in the successful marketing of food products and protects the public from contaminated food.

The 1906 act reflected the willingness of individuals and firms to accept the restriction of certain liberties in exchange for the protection of other rights. Thus, consumers cannot buy and firms cannot sell tainted or adulterated food products. In return for the limitation on their "freedom" to buy or sell, individuals receive greater personal health security, and firms benefit from consumer confidence in their products.

The speculative risks of drug companies are especially high. The pharmaceutical industry develops an estimated 30,000 chemical compounds for each one approved for prescription use. As one research institute has noted, "many new drugs are discovered or developed, but few are cleared for marketing." Research, testing, and FDA approval frequently require a decade before a new product enters the market; thus, returns on investment are extremely delayed, and once on the market, drugs may have only seven or eight years of the seventeen-year patent life remaining. And, even more likely, they may be replaced on the shelf by a new product from a competitor. Nevertheless, such delays in market approval serve the purpose of providing greater assurances of the safety and effectiveness of drugs. Ironically, early release to the markets of other countries can provide evidence of problems if any develop. On the other hand, delayed release increases costs, can contribute to the perpetuation of suffering or illness, and can also indirectly create real economic loss. Current debates over FDA regulations generally concern methods of expediting or improving testing and release rather than the question of whether the agency should or should not regulate.

GO ON TO THE NEXT PAGE

53. What is the main idea of the passage?
    (A) Thousands of drugs are constantly being developed.
    (B) The FDA plays a critical role in approving new drugs.
    (C) Many individuals desire greater freedom in buying and selling food and drug products
    (D) The FDA should be abolished.

54. It can be inferred that the FDA was most likely created because
    (A) only the government can prevent unsanitary food conditions
    (B) some industries were operating under unsanitary conditions
    (C) many industries were opposed to sanitation measures
    (D) death from food poisoning was rampant prior to 1906

55. Discussions about FDA regulations are generally concerned with which of the following?
    (A) Whether the agency should regulate drugs
    (B) Improved testing and release of drugs
    (C) Competition from other countries
    (D) Extending the current patent agreement

56. According to the passage, approximately how many years does it take to bring a new drug to market?
    (A) 1
    (B) 7 to 8
    (C) 10
    (D) 17

GO ON TO THE NEXT PAGE

Questions 57–60

The principal choice in typewriters today is between the electric and the electronic models. The electronic typewriter appears to be the direction of the future. By 1984 sales of electronic machines had already surpassed those of electric models. The fundamental difference between electric and electronic models is that electric typewriters use numerous mechanically driven parts, whereas electronic models have fewer parts (hence less breakage) and function by means of microprocessor controls. In addition, electric typewriters have no memory, display, or automated functions. As the cost of electronic models declines and their superior capabilities become more widely known, they will become even more popular and more widely used.

Electronic typewriters were introduced in 1978 and since then have advanced technologically to compete successfully not only with electric typewriters but, in many cases, with more expensive word processors and computers. The features of electronic typewriters vary from one model to another, but most have a memory feature that enables users to store a certain amount of text that can be recalled later.

This and other features (such as memory protection, pitch selection, right-margin justification, and automatic hyphenation) amount to less work for the user, faster and easier production (up to 50-percent increase in performance), more accurate and attractive results, and generally more efficient office operations. Business analysts predict that in the coming decade electronic typewriters will be used primarily in secretarial-administrative work stations in large companies, but will also be widely used throughout small and medium-size firms.

57. According to the passage, what is the fundamental difference between electric and electronic typewriters?
    (A) Cost
    (B) Number of parts
    (C) Number of models available
    (D) Size

58. According to the passage, features on electronic typewriters are
    (A) likely to be modified within a short period of time
    (B) similar to those on an electric typewriter
    (C) difficult to learn
    (D) likely to increase a user's performance

GO ON TO THE NEXT PAGE

59. The author predicts that electronic typewriters will become more widely used when
    (A) their price comes down
    (B) they have more features
    (C) their memory capacity is increased
    (D) most electric typewriters have broken down

60. The author would most likely agree with which of the following statements?
    (A) The electronic typewriter is superior to the electric typewriter.
    (B) The electric typewriter is superior to the electronic typewriter.
    (C) Both typewriters are equal.
    (D) The two typewriters cannot be compared.

THIS IS THE END OF SECTION 3

IF YOU FINISH BEFORE TIME IS CALLED, CHECK YOUR WORK
ON SECTION 3 ONLY.
DO NOT READ OR WORK ON ANY OTHER SECTION OF THE TEST.

STOP   STOP   STOP   **STOP**   STOP   STOP   STOP

PRACTICE TEST 2

SECTION 1
LISTENING COMPREHENSION

The questions in Section 1 of the test are on a recording.

In this section of the test, you will have an opportunity to demonstrate your ability to understand spoken English. There are three parts to this section, with special directions for each part.

Part A

Directions: For each question in Part A, you will hear a short sentence. Each sentence will be spoken just one time. The sentence you hear will not be written out for you. Therefore, you must listen carefully to understand what the speaker says.

After you hear a sentence, read the four choices in your test book, marked (A), (B), (C), and (D), and decide which *one* is closest in meaning to the sentence you heard. Then, on your answer sheet, find the number of the question and fill in the space that matches the letter of the answer you have chosen. Fill in the space so that the letter inside the oval cannot be seen.

Example I   **Sample Answer**
  You will hear: *Mary swam out to the island with her*   Ⓐ Ⓑ ● Ⓓ
                         friends.
  You will read: (A) Mary outswam the others.
                       (B) Mary ought to swim with them.
                       (C) Mary and her friends swam to the island.
                       (D) Mary's friends owned the island.

The speaker said, "Mary swam out to the island with her friends." Sentence (C), "Mary and her friends swam to the island," is closest in meaning to the sentence you heard. Therefore, you should choose answer (C).

Example II   **Sample Answer**
  You will hear: *Would you mind helping me with this load*   Ⓐ ● Ⓒ Ⓓ
                         of books?
  You will read: (A) Please remind me to read this book.
                       (B) Could you help me carry these books?
                       (C) I don't mind if you help me.
                       (D) Do you have a heavy course load?

The speaker said, "Would you mind helping me with this load of books?" Sentence (B), "Could you help me carry these books?" is closest in meaning to the sentence you heard. Therefore, you should choose answer (B).

GO ON TO THE NEXT PAGE

1. (A) Where are you?
   (B) What road did you take?
   (C) How long did it take?
   (D) What took you so long?

2. (A) The newspaper comes every two days.
   (B) I need a receipt for the paper.
   (C) I have two newspapers.
   (D) The paper hasn't been delivered for two days.

3. (A) There are only four chapters in the book.
   (B) The examination is on top of the book.
   (C) First, I'll read all four chapters.
   (D) The test will cover Chapters 1–4.

4. (A) Eat a little something if you feel hungry.
   (B) Don't eat before dinner time.
   (C) If you don't eat, you'll be hungry.
   (D) Why don't you wait until dinner?

5. (A) Ten of us went by taxi.
   (B) The airport is ten miles from town.
   (C) We spent ten dollars to take the taxi to the airport.
   (D) The taxi from the airport cost ten dollars.

6. (A) How often do you go riding?
   (B) How long is the ride?
   (C) Would you like to go in the car this afternoon?
   (D) Are you leaving at noon?

7. (A) I have to do housework this weekend.
   (B) I have to stay home and study.
   (C) I always go out on Saturdays.
   (D) I didn't have to work this weekend.

8. (A) The train is ten minutes late.
   (B) The plane will be here in ten minutes.
   (C) It will rain before we go.
   (D) The grain was loaded long ago.

9. (A) I'll phone you after I wake up.
   (B) I walked to the phone booth.
   (C) I was asleep before the phone rang.
   (D) I didn't hear the phone ring.

10. (A) The park was preserved by the faculty.
    (B) The facility was planned for visitors.
    (C) Visitors must have a reservation.
    (D) Only staff members and visitors may park in these spaces.

11. (A) Did the books belong to Richard?
    (B) Is Richard going to the library?
    (C) Did Richard take the books back to the library?
    (D) Are these the books Richard returned to the library?

GO ON TO THE NEXT PAGE

12. (A) The statue is two blocks on the right.
    (B) Walk until you see the statue.
    (C) Make two right turns and you'll see the statue.
    (D) At the statue, turn right and go two more blocks.

13. (A) Approximately 2,000 people will attend the conference.
    (B) We counted a thousand people at the conference.
    (C) We expect you will attend the conference.
    (D) The conference was last weekend.

14. (A) The news is over at 6 every evening.
    (B) I never miss the newscast at 6.
    (C) I usually watch the news between 4 and 6.
    (D) Channel Six shows the news at 4.

15. (A) I ordered a telephone last week.
    (B) The phone's been broken for a week.
    (C) My loan was due last week.
    (D) I asked for a loan last week.

16. (A) They're building a three-story office.
    (B) A fire began on the third floor.
    (C) They broke the door on the third floor.
    (D) The fire spread throughout the building.

17. (A) Mr. Johnson fell asleep at 10.
    (B) Mr. Johnson went to bed after midnight.
    (C) Mr. Johnson slept until midnight.
    (D) Mr. Johnson was in bed by 10.

18. (A) The restaurant is next to the movie.
    (B) We'll watch a movie after we eat.
    (C) Before moving, we must get something to eat.
    (D) Let's buy some food before we leave.

19. (A) All schools require good grades.
    (B) The best schools won't admit me.
    (C) I get good grades in school.
    (D) I got my best grades in high school.

20. (A) The rain killed the grass.
    (B) We need less rain.
    (C) Rain water filled the glass.
    (D) The lawn needs water.

GO ON TO THE NEXT PAGE

Part B

Directions: In Part B you will hear short conversations between two speakers. At the end of each conversation, a third person will ask a question about what was said. You will hear each conversation and question about it just one time. The sentence you hear will not be written out for you. Therefore, you must listen carefully to understand what the speaker says. After you hear a conversation and the question about it, read the four possible answers in your test book and decide which *one* is the best answer to the question you heard. Then, on your answer sheet, find the number of the question and fill in the space that matches the letter of the answer you have chosen.

Example   **Sample Answer**

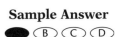

You will hear:
(**first man**) *Professor Smith is going to retire soon. What kind of gift shall we give her?*
(**woman**) *I think she'd like to have a photograph of our class.*
(**second man**) *What does the woman think the class should do?*
You will read: (A) Present Professor Smith with a picture.
(B) Photograph Professor Smith.
(C) Put glass over the photograph.
(D) Replace the broken headlight.

From the conversation you learn that the woman thinks Professor Smith would like a photograph of the class. The best answer to the question "What does the woman think the class should do?" is (A), "Present Professor Smith with a picture." Therefore, you should choose answer (A).

21. (A) Mrs. Smith is always on time.
    (B) They need to turn on the furnace.
    (C) It's hot in the building.
    (D) He was expecting Mrs. Smith this morning.

22. (A) Math.
    (B) Reading.
    (C) English.
    (D) History.

23 (A) His keys.
    (B) His glasses.
    (C) His book.
    (D) His briefcase.

24. (A) She doesn't like to read.
    (B) She already finished it.
    (C) She doesn't have a watch.
    (D) She's very busy.

25. (A) In a department store.
    (B) In a post office.
    (C) In a lamp store.
    (D) In a supermarket.

26. (A) Schools won't accept him.
    (B) He wants to travel more.
    (C) He gets too much mail.
    (D) His school isn't good enough.

GO ON TO THE NEXT PAGE ▶

27. (A) At a bus stop.
    (B) At a cinema.
    (C) At a bank.
    (D) At a clothing store.

28. (A) He prefers milk and sugar.
    (B) He's sorry he caused so much trouble.
    (C) He doesn't want too much sugar.
    (D) He doesn't want coffee.

29. (A) To a gas station.
    (B) To an air conditioning repair shop.
    (C) To a stationery store.
    (D) To a sporting goods store.

30. (A) She did well on the test.
    (B) The test was easy.
    (C) She earned a lot of money.
    (D) She's going away for awhile.

31. (A) He doesn't plan to write the paper.
    (B) He doesn't like to sleep.
    (C) The book is overdue.
    (D) He'll finish the paper tonight.

32. (A) She's rearranging furniture.
    (B) She has a bad back.
    (C) She can't open the window.
    (D) She's buying a new desk.

33. (A) Cancel a trip.
    (B) Buy a car.
    (C) Return a car.
    (D) Purchase a ticket.

34. (A) One night.
    (B) A week.
    (C) Four weeks.
    (D) Four months.

35. (A) She prefers taxis.
    (B) She doesn't have enough money.
    (C) She doesn't have exact change.
    (D) She thinks the cab will be faster.

GO ON TO THE NEXT PAGE

Part C

Directions: In this part of the test, you will hear short talks and conversations. After each of them, you will be asked some questions. You will hear the talks and conversations just one time. They will not be written out for you. Therefore, you must listen carefully in order to understand what the speaker says.

After you hear a question, read the four possible answers in your test book and decide which one is the best answer to the question you heard. Then, on your answer sheet, find the number of the question and fill in the space that matches the letter of the answer you have chosen.

Answer all questions on the basis of what is *stated* or *implied* in the talk or conversation.

Listen to this sample talk.
   You will hear:
      (first man)   *Balloons have been used for about a hundred years. There are two kinds of sport balloons, gas and hot air. Hot-air balloons are safer than gas balloons, which may catch fire. Hot-air balloons are preferred by most balloonists in the United States because of their safety. They are also cheaper and easier to manage than gas balloons. Despite the ease of operating a balloon, pilots must watch the weather carefully. Sport balloon flights are best early in the morning or late in the afternoon, when the wind is light.*

Now look at the following example.   **Sample Answer**
   You will hear: Ⓐ ● Ⓒ Ⓓ
      (second man)   *Why are gas balloons considered dangerous?*
   You will read: (A) They are impossible to guide.
                         (B) They may go up in flames.
                         (C) They tend to leak gas.
                         (D) They are cheaply made.
   The best answer to the question "Why are gas balloons considered dangerous?" is (B), "They may go up in flames." Therefore, you should choose answer (B).

GO ON TO THE NEXT PAGE

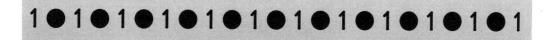
Now look at the next example.

You will hear:

(second man)   *According to the speaker, what must balloon pilots be careful to do?*

Sample Answer

● Ⓑ Ⓒ Ⓓ

You will read: (A) Watch for changes in weather.
(B) Watch their altitude.
(C) Check for weak spots in their balloons.
(D) Test the strength of the ropes.

The best answer to the question "According to the speaker, what must balloon pilots be careful to do?" is (A), "Watch for changes in weather." Therefore, you should choose answer (A).

36. (A) Their lack of water.
(B) Their extra helium.
(C) Their density.
(D) Their lack of oxygen.

37. (A) It is denser.
(B) It is not as light.
(C) It can be released by heating.
(D) It cannot be extracted.

38. (A) In Colorado.
(B) In lowland areas.
(C) Below the lunar surface.
(D) On highland plateaus.

39. (A) Meteorites.
(B) Low levels of oxygen.
(C) Lava.
(D) Fusion of the rocks.

40. (A) In Hawaii.
(B) In Iowa.
(C) In Swaziland.
(D) In the eastern United States.

41. (A) Travel agents.
(B) Common people.
(C) The government.
(D) The industrial sector.

42. (A) Red is a prettier color.
(B) More people want red ones.
(C) Red is cheaper to produce.
(D) Red is very elegant.

43. (A) Children.
(B) Civil groups.
(C) Our changing income.
(D) Working parents.

44. (A) The introduction of the jet plane.
(B) The inconvenient schedule.
(C) The lack of comfort.
(D) The quality of advertisements.

GO ON TO THE NEXT PAGE

45. (A) Demand for train service.
    (B) Government support.
    (C) Better workers
    (D) Elegant service.

46. (A) Like a snapshot.
    (B) A good investment.
    (C) A popular art form.
    (D) An established fashion.

47. (A) More interesting.
    (B) More expensive.
    (C) Better quality.
    (D) More in demand.

48. (A) Museum collections.
    (B) Price.
    (C) Fashion.
    (D) Artist's reputation.

49. (A) Informal.
    (B) Inexpensive.
    (C) Stylized.
    (D) Fashionable.

50. (A) By price.
    (B) By resale value.
    (C) By fad.
    (D) By size.

THIS IS THE END OF THE LISTENING COMPREHENSION SECTION OF THE TEST

THE NEXT PART OF THE TEST IS SECTION 2. TURN TO THE
DIRECTIONS FOR SECTION 2 IN YOUR TEST BOOK. READ THEM,
AND BEGIN WORK. DO NOT READ OR WORK ON ANY OTHER
SECTION OF THE TEST.

SECTION 2
STRUCTURE AND WRITTEN EXPRESSION
Time: 25 minutes

This section tests your ability to recognize language that is appropriate for standard written English. There are two types of questions in this section, with special directions for each type.

Directions: Questions 1–15 are incomplete sentences. Beneath each sentence, you will see four words or phrases, marked (A), (B), (C), and (D). Choose the *one* word or phrase that best completes the sentence. Then, on your answer sheet, find the number of the question and fill in the space that corresponds to the letter of the answer you have chosen. Fill in the space so that the letter inside the oval cannot be seen.

Example I

Vegetables are an excellent source _____ vitamins.
(A) of
(B) has
(C) where
(D) that

Sample Answer

The sentence should read, "Vegetables are an excellent source of vitamins." Therefore, you should choose answer (A).

Example II

_____ in history when remarkable progress was made within a relatively short span of time.
(A) Periods
(B) Throughout periods
(C) There have been periods
(D) Periods have been

Sample Answer

The sentence should read, "There have been periods in history when remarkable progress was made within a relatively short span of time." Therefore, you should choose answer (C).

Now begin work on the questions.

1. With a few exceptions, a passport is required _____ all U.S. citizens who depart and enter the United States.
   (A) to
   (B) with
   (C) of
   (D) at

2. The first large-scale migration from the Old World to the New _____ during the last ice age, around 11,500 years ago.
   (A) have been happening
   (B) happened
   (C) was happened
   (D) happening

3. To early man, the distinction _____ animate and inanimate objects was not always obvious.
   (A) from
   (B) among
   (C) with
   (D) between

4. In order to win a plurality, a candidate must receive _____ votes than anyone running against him or her.
   (A) a greater number of
   (B) of greater number
   (C) greater number of
   (D) of a greater number

5. Few major advances in science have been the work of only _____ person.
   (A) some
   (B) any
   (C) the
   (D) one

6. Most foods have more than one nutrient, but _____ provides all the essential nutrients.
   (A) single no food
   (B) no single food
   (C) food no single
   (D) no food single

7. During the meeting, the leaders agreed _____ ambassadors and renew cultural contacts.
   (A) exchanging
   (B) exchange
   (C) to exchange
   (D) for exchanging

8. Robert Goddard is generally acknowledged _____ the father of modern rocketry.
   (A) being
   (B) to be
   (C) who is
   (D) is

9. Rhode Island, _____ of the 50 states, is densely populated and highly industrialized.
   (A) small
   (B) the small
   (C) smaller
   (D) the smallest

10. After a one-year cruise, an unmanned spacecraft will arrive at and _____ orbiting Mars.
    (A) begin to
    (B) to begin
    (C) has began
    (D) begin

11. About 500 volcanoes have had recorded eruptions within _____ times.
    (A) history
    (B) historically
    (C) historian
    (D) historical

12. The _____ geological history of the Earth since the beginning of the Cambrian Period is subdivided into three eras.
    (A) knowing
    (B) knew
    (C) known
    (D) know

13. _____ provides more income and jobs than any other segment of the economy.
    (A) To manufacture
    (B) Manufacturing
    (C) Manufactured
    (D) Being manufactured

14. Since 1958, the United States has consumed more energy than it _____.
    (A) producing
    (B) has produced
    (C) produced
    (D) production

15. The seasons _____ by the tilt of the Earth's axis.
    (A) cause
    (B) are causing
    (C) are caused
    (D) caused

GO ON TO THE NEXT PAGE

Directions: In questions 16–40, each sentence has four underlined words or phrases. The four underlined parts of the sentence are marked (A), (B), (C), and (D). Identify the *one* underlined word or phrase that must be changed in order for the sentence to be correct. Then, on your answer sheet, find the number of the question and fill in the space that corresponds to the letter of the answer you have chosen.

Example I   **Sample Answer**
                                                                 Ⓐ Ⓑ ● Ⓓ

A ray of light passing <u>through</u> <u>the center</u> of a thin lens <u>keep</u>
                        A   **B**   **C**

its <u>original</u> direction.
     D

The sentence should read, "A ray of light passing through the center of a thin lens keeps its original direction." Therefore, you should choose answer (C).

Example II   **Sample Answer**
                                                                 Ⓐ Ⓑ Ⓒ ●

The mandolin, a musical <u>instrument</u> <u>that has</u> strings, was probably copied
                          A   **B**

<u>from</u> the lute, a <u>many</u> older instrument.
 C   **D**

The sentence should read, "The mandolin, a musical instrument that has strings, was probably copied from the lute, a much older instrument." Therefore, you should choose answer (D).

Now begin work on the questions.

16. <u>Highly</u> prices <u>for</u> food <u>result</u> from middlemen <u>who</u> make a profit from the
      A   **B**   **C**   **D**
     farmer's crops.

17. Since little rain falls <u>in</u> the desert, plants <u>need to be</u> conserve <u>whatever</u> water
                             A   **B**   **C**
     <u>they can</u>.
       D

18. The Boy Scout organization <u>stresses</u> outdoor knowledge <u>and</u> <u>training citizenship.</u>
    A   B   C   D

19. Broadway, <u>the famous</u> thoroughfare of New York city, <u>is</u> the <u>most long</u> street
               A   B   C

    <u>in the world.</u>
    D

20. The President <u>annual</u> <u>submits</u> <u>a</u> budget <u>to</u> Congress in January.
                   A   B   C   D

21. Butter should <u>contain</u> at least 80 <u>percents fat</u> and <u>no more than</u>
                   A   B   C

    15 percent <u>water.</u>
               D

22. <u>Buttons,</u> originally <u>made of</u> bronze or bone, are now <u>usual</u> made of <u>plastic.</u>
    A   B   C   D

23. California's pleasant climate and <u>beauty natural</u> <u>have</u> attracted great <u>numbers</u>
                                      A   B   C

    of <u>retired</u> persons.
       D

24. <u>Financial contributions</u> to politicians by <u>individuals</u> and corporations <u>restricted</u>
    A   B   C

    <u>by law.</u>
    D

25. In 1901, the Library of Congress <u>began</u> the practice of printing their catalog
                                      A

    entries <u>on</u> small cards and <u>to sell</u> <u>them</u> to other libraries.
            B   C   D

26. Cattle were first <u>brought</u> to the Western Hemisphere <u>by</u> Columbus on <u>his</u>
                      A   B   C

    <u>twice</u> voyage.
    D

GO ON TO THE NEXT PAGE

27. American <u>films which were</u> first made <u>in</u> New York City, <u>but</u> by 1913
      A   **B**   **C**

  Hollywood, California became <u>the movie</u> capital.
           D

28. Although geologists <u>studying</u> earthquakes have refined <u>his</u> predictions in <u>recent</u>
       A   **B**   **C**

  years, they still cannot <u>determine</u> the exact date of a quake.
          D

29. The <u>establishment</u> of large <u>national parks</u> in the early 1900s <u>provide</u> an
     A   **B**   **C**

  additional source of revenue <u>through</u> the tourist trade.
          D

30. The <u>sudden</u> melting of snow or ice <u>are</u> <u>a primary</u> cause <u>of flooding</u>.
    A   **B** **C**   **D**

31. The <u>invented</u> of the telegraph made <u>possible</u> almost <u>instantaneous</u> <u>communication</u>.
    A   **B**   **C**   **D**

32. The computer that <u>developed</u> from the calculating machine <u>it</u> could <u>perform</u>
        A   **B**   **C**

  only one operation <u>at a time</u>.
        D

33. Grain <u>is</u> easy <u>handle</u> and, because of <u>its</u> low water content, it can <u>be</u> stored for
    A **B**   **C**   **D**

  long periods.

34. Babies, <u>on the average</u>, double their <u>weight</u> at six months of age, and <u>triple it</u> by
      A   **B**   **C**

  <u>her</u> first birthday.
  D

35. Fossil records indicate <u>that many</u> insect species <u>exist today</u> in much the same
          A   **B**

  form <u>as</u> they <u>do</u> 200 million years ago.
    C **D**

GO ON TO THE NEXT PAGE

36. Some <u>physicians practice</u> medicine as a group <u>so that specialized</u> treatment will
               A   **B**

    be <u>availability</u> at a <u>lower</u> cost.
          C   **D**

37. For many <u>industrial</u> <u>uses</u>, the <u>melting</u> points of metal <u>is</u> important when
             A   **B**   **C**   **D**

    selecting alloys for a compound.

38. Pottery, <u>the oldest</u> and most widespread art form, <u>was</u> one of the most <u>enduring</u>
          A   **B**   **C**

    materials <u>to know</u> to man.
            D

39. <u>Private mail</u> companies <u>have begun</u> to replace the long <u>establishing</u> public
      A   **B**   **C**

    <u>postal</u> system.
     D

40. Most <u>color blind</u> people <u>finds</u> it <u>difficult</u> to <u>identify</u> red or green.
       A   **B**   **C**   **D**

THIS IS THE END OF SECTION 2

IF YOU FINISH BEFORE TIME IS CALLED, CHECK YOUR WORK
ON SECTION 2 ONLY.
DO NOT READ OR WORK ON ANY OTHER SECTION OF THE TEST.
THE SUPERVISOR WILL TELL YOU WHEN TO BEGIN WORK
ON SECTION 3.

SECTION 3
VOCABULARY AND READING COMPREHENSION
Time: 45 minutes

This section tests your comprehension of standard written English. There are two types of questions in this section, with special directions for each type.

Directions: In questions 1–30, each sentence has an underlined word or phrase. Below each sentence are four other words or phrases, marked (A), (B), (C), and (D). You are to choose the *one* word or phrase that *best keeps the meaning* of the original sentence if it is substituted for the underlined word or phrase. Then, on your answer sheet, find the number of the question and fill in the space that matches the letter you have chosen. Fill in the space so that the letter inside the oval cannot be seen.

Example

Passenger ships and <u>aircraft</u> are often equipped with ship-to-shore or air-to-land radio telephones.
(A)   highways
(B)   railroads
(C)   planes
(D)   sailboats

Sample Answer
Ⓐ Ⓑ ● Ⓓ

The best answer is (C), because "Passenger ships and planes are often equipped with ship-to-shore or air-to-land radio telephones" is closest in meaning to the original sentence. Therefore, you should choose answer (C).

Now begin work on the questions.

1. Rivers provide a <u>link</u> between inland areas and the sea.
    (A)   force
    (B)   portal
    (C)   connection
    (D)   canal

2. Rival companies <u>compete</u> to produce a better product at a lower price.
    (A)   battle
    (B)   endeavor
    (C)   work
    (D)   continue

3. The quality and <u>scope</u> of hospital care vary in different parts of the world.
    (A)   value
    (B)   form
    (C)   expense
    (D)   range

4. It is the job of the labor unions to negotiate <u>contracts</u> for their members.
    (A)   written agreements
    (B)   vacation time
    (C)   health benefits
    (D)   new jobs

GO ON TO THE NEXT PAGE

5. The 1920s have generally been considered a decade of growth and prosperity.
   (A) happiness
   (B) reform
   (C) success
   (D) stabilization

6. Heavy grazing by cattle reduces the amount of rainwater that soil can absorb.
   (A) tolerate
   (B) release
   (C) extract
   (D) take in

7. Considerable amounts of the Earth's fresh water are frozen in polar ice caps and glaciers.
   (A) Large
   (B) Increasing
   (C) Negligible
   (D) Sufficient

8. Many common household materials can produce toxic fumes.
   (A) poisonous
   (B) sweet
   (C) cleansing
   (D) odorous

9. Artificial reefs are successful in hiding small fish from predators.
   (A) Underwater
   (B) Dense
   (C) Shallow
   (D) Synthetic

10. Amateur athletes of many nations compete in the Olympic Games.
    (A) Qualified
    (B) Exceptional
    (C) Youthful
    (D) Nonprofessional

11. The United States has 25 percent of the world's available coal reserves.
    (A) hidden
    (B) mined
    (C) valuable
    (D) accessible

12. Studies have shown that diets high in fat increase the risk of heart disease.
    (A) incidence
    (B) danger
    (C) damage
    (D) rate

13. Forestry researchers speculate that trees communicate in some fashion.
    (A) prove
    (B) guess
    (C) predict
    (D) deny

14. Volcanoes are formed when molten rock erupts from the ground.
    (A) bursts
    (B) seeps
    (C) oozes
    (D) leaks

GO ON TO THE NEXT PAGE

15. Experiments are often <u>conducted</u> in a laboratory under controlled conditions.
    (A) discussed
    (B) performed
    (C) debated
    (D) started

16. A plant's protective tissue forms an outer layer in order to <u>reduce</u> water loss.
    (A) promote
    (B) contain
    (C) diminish
    (D) delay

17. As water <u>vapor</u> rises, it cools.
    (A) temperature
    (B) level
    (C) mist
    (D) density

18. The Atmosphere is 350 miles <u>thick</u> and is held to Earth by gravity.
    (A) high
    (B) dense
    (C) long
    (D) away

19. Climate is <u>affected</u> by a region's altitude.
    (A) determined
    (B) measured
    (C) regulated
    (D) influenced

20. The <u>main</u> source of energy in the United States today is oil.
    (A) principal
    (B) original
    (C) most abundant
    (D) most expensive

21. At the current rate of <u>consumption</u>, fossil fuels will probably run out within the next few hundred years.
    (A) use
    (B) contamination
    (C) isolation
    (D) waste

22. Nuclear engineers find it difficult to <u>dispose of</u> radioactive wastes in a safe manner.
    (A) produce
    (B) dissolve
    (C) discard
    (D) purchase

23. Body language <u>conveys</u> shades of meaning that words alone cannot express.
    (A) convenes
    (B) determines
    (C) transmits
    (D) hides

24. In office buildings, artificial light provides more <u>uniform</u> illumination than natural light.
    (A) consistent
    (B) bright
    (C) diffused
    (D) ambient

GO ON TO THE NEXT PAGE

25. The <u>diversity</u> of New York's population creates an exciting environment.
    (A) strength
    (B) quality
    (C) position
    (D) variety

26. Technology has provided a way to recycle water and <u>purify</u> it.
    (A) chill
    (B) sell
    (C) clean
    (D) store

27. The diet of more than one-tenth of the world's population cannot <u>sustain</u> a person's health.
    (A) damage
    (B) improve
    (C) maintain
    (D) alter

28. Scientific dating <u>techniques</u> cannot reveal the age of molten rocks.
    (A) methods
    (B) equipment
    (C) experiments
    (D) data

29. Industrial growth was <u>spurred</u> by the use of electricity.
    (A) caused
    (B) guaranteed
    (C) stimulated
    (D) created

30. Acid rain <u>presently</u> threatens many major forests of the northeastern United States.
    (A) currently
    (B) usually
    (C) continually
    (D) accidently

GO ON TO THE NEXT PAGE

Directions: In the rest of this section you will read several passages. Each one is followed by several questions about it. For questions 31–60, you are to choose the *one* best answer, (A), (B), (C), or (D), to each question. Then, on your answer sheet, find the number of the question and fill in the space that matches the letter of the answer you have chosen.

Answer all questions following a passage on the basis of what is *stated* or *implied* in the reading passage.

Example passage and questions

The rattles with which a rattlesnake warns of its presence are formed by loosely interlocking hollow rings of hard skin, which make a buzzing sound when its tail is shaken. As a baby, the snake begins to form its rattles from the button at the very tip of its tail. Thereafter, each time it sheds its skin, a new ring is formed. Popular belief holds that a snake's age can be told by counting the rings, but this idea is fallacious. In fact, a snake may lose its old skin as often as four times a year. Also, rattles tend to wear or break off with time.

Example I

A rattlesnake's rattles are made of

(A) skin
(B) bone
(C) wood
(D) muscle

Sample Answer

According to the passage, a rattlesnake's rattles are made of rings of hard skin. Therefore, you should choose answer (A).

Example II

How often does a rattlesnake shed its skin?

(A) Once every four years
(B) Once every four months
(C) Up to four times every year
(D) Four times more often than other snakes

Sample Answer

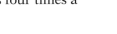

The passage states that "a snake may lose its old skin as often as four times a year." Therefore, you should choose answer (C).

Now begin work on the questions.

GO ON TO THE NEXT PAGE

Questions 31–35

Many Americans aspire to "be their own boss." These aspirations became realities after 1945 with the boom in franchising. A franchise allows an individual to do business under the name and corporate image of a national firm. One of the world's best-known examples of a franchise is McDonald's Restaurants.

In return for the use of the corporate name and products, small-business entrepreneurs agree to operate in a prescribed manner. They can sell only the specified products. They have to pay an initial fee for the franchise, and they have to return to the franchiser a percentage of the sales. The franchise holders often obtain capital to start the business from the national corporation. Thus, the risk of entering a new business is somewhat reduced. Initially the capital required for most franchises was relatively small. However, in the 1980s, some large franchises required an investment of over half a million dollars.

When fast-food franchises became popular, franchises also emerged in electronics, bookstores, handicrafts, toys, clothing and many other product lines and services. The spread of these small franchised businesses dramatically altered the marketing of some products. In the case of the fast-food industry, franchises also altered American dietary patterns.

31. What is the main subject of the passage?
    (A) American businesspeople are independent.
    (B) Franchises are an easy way to success.
    (C) Franchises have helped many Americans to start businesses.
    (D) Eating habits changed in 1945.

32. Which of the following can be inferred as the primary reason that franchising was successful?
    (A) People preferred to be their own boss.
    (B) The heads of large corporations wanted greater profits.
    (C) Franchising was more profitable than independent business.
    (D) Consumers wanted consistency.

GO ON TO THE NEXT PAGE

33. The franchising of the fast-food business altered which of the following:
    (A) Corporate salaries
    (B) The nature of franchising
    (C) Many companies' corporate images
    (D) People's eating habits

34. According to the passage, which franchise promoted the growth of other franchises?
    (A) Fast food
    (B) Electronics
    (C) Bookstores
    (D) Toys

35. According to the passage, what is the main difference between the early and more recent days of franchising?
    (A) It cost nothing to use the corporate name in the early days.
    (B) Most of the early franchise made modest profits in the early days.
    (C) The initial investment is much higher in recent days.
    (D) The American public is more aware of franchises in recent days.

GO ON TO THE NEXT PAGE

Questions 36–41

The foreign policy of the United States in the 1920s and 1930s could be called isolationism. After World War I, war had lost its glamour. The invention of the movie camera in the 1930s made the horrors of war vividly real to millions of Americans.

For generations, a peace movement had existed in the United States. It had always
5 been relatively ineffectual, but now it grew to heights of unexampled influence. One wing argued strongly for the United States to prevent war by acting on the principle of collective security; that is, by banding together with other nations to present a common front to the aggressors. Other more radical groups—like the War Resister's League—preached isolationism. The League of Nations, they said, was weak;
10 militarism was taking over everywhere, and the only answer was to refuse to build armaments and follow totally noninterventionist policies.

36. According to the passage, the early peace movement had been
    (A) isolated
    (B) very influential
    (C) fairly ineffectual
    (D) conservative

37. According to the passage, it can be inferred that the War Resister's League did NOT support which of the following?
    (A) Isolationism
    (B) Militarism
    (C) The peace movement
    (D) The principle of collective security

38. With which of the following is the passage mainly concerned?
    (A) Glamour
    (B) First World War
    (C) Isolationism
    (D) War Resister's League

39. The author uses the expression "unexampled influence" (line 5) to imply that
    (A) the cause was not influential
    (B) no one could succeed
    (C) there was no precedent
    (D) peace was unattainable

40. The groups referred to in the last paragraph were against which of the following?
    (A) Intervention
    (B) War
    (C) Collective security
    (D) Isolationism

41. Which of the following argued that military armaments should not be built?
    (A) The British press
    (B) The War Resister's League
    (C) The League of Nations
    (D) The aggressors

GO ON TO THE NEXT PAGE

Questions 42–46

A number of artists in the past have practiced architecture, sculpture, and painting. For instance, in 16th-century Italy there was no feeling that it was improper to work in all three areas, and in the case of Michelangelo it would be difficult to determine in which discipline he was preeminent.

Today such a thing would be almost impossible. It has become common practice to specialize in painting or sculpture, occasionally to engage in both, but never to encompass all three disciplines. One of the obvious reasons is that training in architecture now involves so much technical instruction that demands of time exclude other studies. Thus, a historical link between the three arts has been broken. At least one unfortunate effect of this break is that the architect, who is frequently the purchaser of painting and sculpture for an architectural setting, may have an undeveloped pictorial and sculptural sensitivity, which may make his or her choices less than appropriate.

The most significant effect of the separation perhaps has been that painting and sculpture have come to be regarded as different from architecture, and when the fine arts are considered, it is these areas that are usually referred to. But painting and sculpture are as different in kind from each other as both are from architecture.

Sculpture has a long history of close connection with architectural structures. The integration of the building with the external sculptures on, say, an Indian temple or the north door of Chartres Cathedral is immediately evident. Because sculpture, like architecture, is generally three-dimensional, their relationship is easily compared.

GO ON TO THE NEXT PAGE

42. The author of the passage would probably agree with which of the following statements?
    (A) Michelangelo would not be popular today.
    (B) An artist could specialize in more than two disciplines.
    (C) An artist could equal Michelangelo in sculpture.
    (D) Architects often desire to become painters.

43. The author mentions Michelangelo for which of the following reasons?
    (A) Michelangelo lived in Italy, where a lot of sculpture was made.
    (B) Michelangelo was a great patron of the arts.
    (C) Michelangelo was proficient in all three art forms.
    (D) Michelangelo worked only in three-dimensional objects.

44. The author of the passage suggests that
    (A) the art of 16th-century Italy is superior to anything being done today
    (B) Michelangelo was the greatest artist that ever lived
    (C) painting and sculpture are unrelated
    (D) modern architects may not be as well-rounded as earlier architects

45. According to the passage, modern architects do not study painting because they
    (A) do not have enough time
    (B) are insensitive
    (C) prefer sculpture
    (D) do not require technical instruction

46. A modern architect's choices of paintings and sculptures might be less than appropriate because the architect
    (A) thinks mainly of profit
    (B) does not have time to study works of art
    (C) may lack sensitivity outside his or her area of expertise
    (D) doesn't have enough money to buy quality works of art

GO ON TO THE NEXT PAGE

Questions 47–52

Two hundred thousand years after the appearance of man, an embryonic language began to develop, replacing a communication based mainly on touch. Regardless of whether this language developed from learning or instinct, genetic evolution had now been joined by language evolution. By about 7,000 B.C., *Homo sapiens* had
5 evolved genetically to its present form, and the ability to communicate had gained another medium: pictographics. These wall etchings inside cave walls and temples remain picture messages that depict life and religious beliefs of these first humans. In the first period from 3,000 to 2,000 B.C. these etchings became highly stylized, and the first symbols came into existence. Primitive alphabets, sometimes consisting of
10 more than 600 characters, marked the beginning of recorded history.

Humans were now able to record sociocultural events, attitudes, values, and habits and to trace the development of moral codes. Many of these techniques continued into modern cultures, such as those of the Native Americans, who recorded famous battles, songs, and the lives of chiefs for posterity. Cultures learned about and
15 studied other cultures. Historical perspectives developed so that when plotting our futures, we could examine our past.

47. The passage mainly discusses which of the following?
   (A) Communication theory
   (B) Styles of writing
   (C) Styles of language
   (D) The early development of language

48. According to the passage, before language was developed, humans communicated by doing which of the following?
   (A) Smoking
   (B) Touching
   (C) Dancing
   (D) Grunting

49. According to the passage, when did the first symbols come into existence?
   (A) 7,000 B.C.
   (B) 2,000 B.C.
   (C) 2,000 years ago
   (D) 600 years ago

50. The word "pictographics" in line 6 refers to which of the following?
   (A) Wall etchings
   (B) Cave walls
   (C) Temple remains
   (D) *Homo sapiens*

51. Recorded history was marked by the existence of which of the following?
   (A) New alphabets
   (B) Cave dwellers
   (C) Moral codes
   (D) Sociocultural events

52. According to the passage, what is the value of historical perspectives?
   (A) To live in the past
   (B) To learn about other cultures
   (C) To develop new moral codes
   (D) To trace our origins

GO ON TO THE NEXT PAGE

Questions 53–56

Although the earliest scientific ideas date back to early recorded history, physics as we know it today began with Galileo Galilei (1564–1642). Indeed, Galileo and his successor Isaac Newton (1642–1727) created a revolution in scientific thought. The physics that developed over the next three centuries, reaching its culmination with
5 the electromagnetic theory of light in the latter half of the 19th century, is now referred to as classical physics. By the turn of the century, it seemed that the physical world was very well understood. But in the early years of the century, new ideas and new experiments in physics indicated that some aspects of classical physics did not work for the tiny world of the atom or for objects traveling at very high speed. This
10 brought on a second great revolution in physics, which gave birth to what is now called modern physics.

The principle aim of all sciences, including physics, is generally considered to be the ordering of the complex appearances detected by our senses—that is, an ordering of what we often refer to as the "world around us." Many people think of science as a
15 mechanical process of collecting facts and devising theories. This is not the case. Science is a creative activity that in many respects resembles other creative activities of the human mind.

53. According to the passage, physics did not begin until
(A) early recorded history
(B) the time of Galileo
(C) the 20th century
(D) the formulation of the electromagnetic theory

54. Which of the following could classical theories of physics NOT explain?
(A) Recorded history
(B) Newon's experiments
(C) The world of the atom
(D) Electromagnetic theory

55. The age of classical physics dated from about
(A) 1564 to 1642
(B) 1564 to 1900
(C) 1850 to 1900
(D) 1642 to 1727

56. The author of the passage defines the "complex appearances detected by our senses" (line 13) as our
(A) eye, ear, and nose
(B) visions of the future
(C) knowledge of physics
(D) environment

GO ON TO THE NEXT PAGE

Questions 57–60

Mass communication does not operate in a social vacuum as a machine does. When a computer receives a message, for instance, it will provide an answer based on that original message. If the computer is functioning properly, the same answer will appear every time we send it the identical message. Now contrast this process with what occurs in mass communication. Imagine that you, a consumer of mass media, read the newspaper story about a politician's speech. After you talked with your family, friends, and co-workers about it, you decided to write a letter to the politician. It is thus possible that three social groups, your family, friends, and co-workers, affected your reaction to the speech.

Now imagine that you are the newspaper responsible for writing about the politician's speech. Social groups will affect your reporting of the story to the public. Perhaps you are a member of a union that goes on strike just as you return to your office to write the story. Or perhaps you belong to a journalism association with a code of reporting ethics to which you personally adhere. The code states that you cannot accept gifts as part of your job as a reporter, and your morning mail brings an invitation from a major oil company to be their guest on a flight to Alaska for an on-the-spot story about oil exploration. You are faced with accepting the free trip and doing the story or rejecting the free trip and permitting other media in your city to obtain the story. You obviously are faced with a dilemma attributable at least in part to the influence various social groups have on you.

57. According to the passage, a human language is unlike an artificial language because it
    (A) has a social element
    (B) is precise
    (C) is more useful
    (D) is complicated

58. What is the main idea of the passage?
    (A) Our reactions are influenced by social groups.
    (B) Alaska is an oil-producing state.
    (C) Communication comes in many forms.
    (D) Reporters should not accept gifts.

GO ON TO THE NEXT PAGE

59. The author of the passage answers which of the following questions?
    (A) How are political speeches received?
    (B) How are your opinions influenced?
    (C) How do you become a newspaper reporter?
    (D) What is the value of a computer?

60. The paragraph following the passage most probably discusses which of the following?
    (A) A code of ethics in journalism
    (B) The role of a computer in society
    (C) The impact of Alaskan oil exploration
    (D) The effect of social influence on mass communication

THIS IS THE END OF SECTION 3

IF YOU FINISH BEFORE TIME IS CALLED, CHECK YOUR WORK
ON SECTION 3 ONLY.
DO NOT READ OR WORK ON ANY OTHER SECTION OF THE TEST.

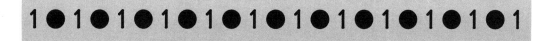

PRACTICE TEST 3

SECTION 1
LISTENING COMPREHENSION

The questions in Section 1 of the test are on a recording.

In this section of the test, you will have an opportunity to demonstrate your ability to understand spoken English. There are three parts to this section, with special directions for each part.

Part A

Directions: For each question in Part A, you will hear a short sentence. Each sentence will be spoken just one time. The sentence you hear will not be written out for you. Therefore, you must listen carefully to understand what the speaker says.

After you hear a sentence, read the four choices in your test book, marked (A), (B), (C), and (D), and decide which *one* is closest in meaning to the sentence you heard. Then, on your answer sheet, find the number of the question and fill in the space that matches the letter of the answer you have chosen. Fill in the space so that the letter inside the oval cannot be seen.

Example I   **Sample Answer**
You will hear: *Mary swam out to the island with her friends.*   Ⓐ Ⓑ ● Ⓓ
You will read: (A) Mary outswam the others.
                     (B) Mary ought to swim with them.
                     (C) Mary and her friends swam to the island.
                     (D) Mary's friends owned the island.

The speaker said, "Mary swam out to the island with her friends." Sentence (C), "Mary and her friends swam to the island," is closest in meaning to the sentence you heard. Therefore, you should choose answer (C).

Example II   **Sample Answer**
You will hear: *Would you mind helping me with this load*   Ⓐ ● Ⓒ Ⓓ
                     of books?
You will read: (A) Please remind me to read this book.
                     (B) Could you help me carry these books?
                     (C) I don't mind if you help me.
                     (D) Do you have a heavy course load?

The speaker said, "Would you mind helping me with this load of books?" Sentence (B), "Could you help me carry these books?" is closest in meaning to the sentence you heard. Therefore, you should choose answer (B).

GO ON TO THE NEXT PAGE

Listening Comprehension **65**

1. (A) The train went through the mountains.
    (B) The birds travelled west.
    (C) The plane flew to Utah.
    (D) Denver is in the mountains.

2. (A) It's been an hour since we first tried.
    (B) Let's try every 30 minutes.
    (C) We've tried for half an hour.
    (D) We'll try again at 12:00.

3. (A) In distress she sat down.
    (B) Her dress was torn.
    (C) She gave her address downtown.
    (D) The store was close to town.

4. (A) The exam wasn't difficult.
    (B) I didn't study.
    (C) It was exactly the same.
    (D) I hadn't studied.

5. (A) The flight was late.
    (B) The flight never arrived.
    (C) Ten Brazilians arrived early at 6:00.
    (D) The flight finally arrived at 7:00

6. (A) The editor saw it first.
    (B) The printer sent it to the editor.
    (C) The editor didn't approve the magazine.
    (D) The little girl was praised for her printing.

7. (A) It was cold.
    (B) We threw them a blanket.
    (C) We didn't need a blanket.
    (D) It was raining.

8. (A) He offered me some raisins.
    (B) He was too angry for a rational discussion.
    (C) He showed me his new play.
    (D) He showed me his list of reasons.

9. (A) I never heard the phone.
    (B) They'll sweep the top story.
    (C) I always cry at stories about orphans.
    (D) I never listen to sad children.

10. (A) All employees were given five prizes.
    (B) The five-year-old won a prize.
    (C) The company was five years old.
    (D) Prizes were given to employees with five years' tenure.

11. (A) Farmers sent bills to the senator's attention.
    (B) Bill lived in the top-floor apartment.
    (C) The rain was only one reason not to go.
    (D) There was a great deal of legislation.

12. (A) The lecture notes were almost blown away by the wind.
    (B) The guests asked for some paper.
    (C) The newspaper reported the speech.
    (D) Strong opinions should not be repeated.

GO ON TO THE NEXT PAGE

13. (A) I arrived at 9:15.
    (B) I got there at 8:45.
    (C) I made my class on time.
    (D) I got up after 9:00.

14. (A) Three power generators will be installed next year.
    (B) People must not use electricity for cooking.
    (C) Demand for power will exceed supply.
    (D) This generation must eat less and reduce.

15. (A) Buildings in earthquake zones need strong support.
    (B) The proof could not have been greater.
    (C) The motion was defeated.
    (D) The motion of the boat made it hard to stand on our feet.

16. (A) The men stood in a row.
    (B) Two soldiers received a promotion.
    (C) The commander stood higher than the others.
    (D) The men's names were on a list.

17. (A) The car ran out of gas during a long race.
    (B) This long sofa is not very functional.
    (C) A problem with the pump shortened the mission.
    (D) They jumped at the chance to stay longer.

18. (A) Mistakes are frequently displayed.
    (B) It was a mistake to advertise.
    (C) They purchased a new monitor.
    (D) Something was typed incorrectly.

19. (A) The gas for the new car is cheaper.
    (B) There is less gas in the new car's tank.
    (C) The gas for my old car was more expensive.
    (D) My new tank is bigger.

20. (A) We wanted to get up early.
    (B) We should have slept more.
    (C) The alarm didn't work.
    (D) We set the alarm for 12:00.

GO ON TO THE NEXT PAGE

Listening Comprehension **67**

Part B

Directions: In Part B you will hear short conversations between two speakers. At the end of each conversation, a third person will ask a question about what was said. You will hear each conversation and question about it just one time. The sentence you hear will not be written out for you. Therefore, you must listen carefully to understand what the speaker says. After you hear a conversation and the question about it, read the four possible answers in your test book and decide which *one* is the best answer to the question you heard. Then, on your answer sheet, find the number of the question and fill in the space that matches the letter of the answer you have chosen.

Example   **Sample Answer**

You will hear:

(first man)   *Professor Smith is going to retire soon. What kind of gift shall we give her?*
(woman)   *I think she'd like to have a photograph of our class.*
(second man)   *What does the woman think the class should do?*
You will read: (A) Present Professor Smith with a picture.
(B) Photograph Professor Smith.
(C) Put glass over the photograph.
(D) Replace the broken headlight.

From the conversation you learn that the woman thinks Professor Smith would like a photograph of the class. The best answer to the question "What does the woman think the class should do?" is (A), "Present Professor Smith with a picture." Therefore, you should choose answer (A).

21. (A) "Sorry to hear that."
     (B) "You've done something wrong."
     (C) "Contacts are no good."
     (D) "Nothing will help."

22. (A) 5 hours.
     (B) 7 hours.
     (C) 9 hours.
     (D) 10 hours.

23. (A) The 4:40 bus.
     (B) The 5:00 bus.
     (C) The 5:20 bus.
     (D) The 5:40 bus.

24. (A) Retired.
     (B) Withdrawn.
     (C) Fatigued.
     (D) Talkative.

GO ON TO THE NEXT PAGE

25. (A) Avoid them.
    (B) Go home.
    (C) Repeat himself.
    (D) Attend a party.

26. (A) Mrs. Smith.
    (B) Her father's family.
    (C) Her husband's family.
    (D) Mr. Smith.

27. (A) The trash taken outside.
    (B) Something for her rash.
    (C) The man to fill the sack.
    (D) For him to get ready.

28. (A) They didn't like the other restaurant.
    (B) He generally eats more than she.
    (C) She eats more than he.
    (D) This is the most they've ever eaten.

29. (A) Go to the mechanic.
    (B) Go to the office.
    (C) Go home.
    (D) Stop for groceries.

30. (A) Thin socks.
    (B) Thick socks.
    (C) New shoes.
    (D) Not enough exercise.

31. (A) The woman.
    (B) Too little sleep.
    (C) A hat.
    (D) The sun.

32. (A) The man's.
    (B) Annie's.
    (C) Bill's.
    (D) Joe's.

33. (A) Tall.
    (B) Short.
    (C) Bald.
    (D) Thin.

34. (A) With a funny story.
    (B) Promptly.
    (C) With a lecture.
    (D) Easily.

35. (A) It's the dullest.
    (B) It's ridiculous.
    (C) It's long.
    (D) It's plain.

GO ON TO THE NEXT PAGE

Part C

Directions: In this part of the test, you will hear short talks and conversations. After each of them, you will be asked some questions. You will hear the talks and conversations just one time. They will not be written out for you. Therefore, you must listen carefully in order to understand what the speaker says.

After you hear a question, read the four possible answers in your test book and decide which *one* is the best answer to the question you heard. Then, on your answer sheet, find the number of the question and fill in the space that matches the letter of the answer you have chosen.

Answer all questions on the basis of what is *stated* or *implied* in the talk or conversation.

Listen to this sample talk.
> **You will hear:**
> **(first man)** *Balloons have been used for about a hundred years. There are two kinds of sport balloons, gas and hot air. Hot-air balloons are safer than gas balloons, which may catch fire. Hot-air balloons are preferred by most balloonists in the United States because of their safety. They are also cheaper and easier to manage than gas balloons. Despite the ease of operating a balloon, pilots must watch the weather carefully. Sport balloon flights are best early in the morning or late in the afternoon, when the wind is light.*

Now look at the following example.

Sample Answer

> **You will hear:**
> **(second man)** *Why are gas balloons considered dangerous?*
> **You will read:** (A) They are impossible to guide.
> (B) They may go up in flames.
> (C) They tend to leak gas.
> (D) They are cheaply made.

The best answer to the question "Why are gas balloons considered dangerous?" is (B), "They may go up in flames." Therefore, you should choose answer (B).

GO ON TO THE NEXT PAGE

Now look at the next example.
You will hear:
(second man) *According to the speaker, what must balloon pilots be careful to do?*
You will read: (A) Watch for changes in weather.
(B) Watch their altitude.
(C) Check for weak spots in their balloons.
(D) Test the strength of the ropes.

Sample Answer
● Ⓑ Ⓒ Ⓓ

The best answer to the question "According to the speaker, what must balloon pilots be careful to do?" is (A), "Watch for changes in weather." Therefore, you should choose answer (A).

36. (A) As popular.
(B) As valuable.
(C) As evil.
(D) As suspicious.

37. (A) Their size.
(B) Their wingspan.
(C) Their echo.
(D) Their eating habits.

38. (A) By sight.
(B) By touch.
(C) By echo.
(D) By instinct.

39. (A) Other bats.
(B) Weather.
(C) Man.
(D) Large mammals.

40. (A) They are very good to eat.
(B) They are valuable mammals.
(C) They live in caves.
(D) They are evil creatures.

41. (A) Ships.
(B) Cars.
(C) Trucks.
(D) Railroads.

42. (A) They're too long.
(B) They have to be maintained.
(C) They are too expensive to build.
(D) There are too few of them.

43. (A) Those with strong navies.
(B) Those with wooden ships.
(C) Those with good roads.
(D) Those with long coastlines.

44. (A) Wide rivers.
(B) High cost of labor.
(C) Availability of forests.
(D) Easy access to China.

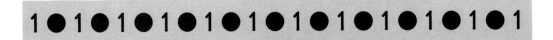

45. (A) Lack of good harbors.
    (B) High cost of shipping construction.
    (C) Too many shipping regulations.
    (D) Increased use of planes.

46. (A) Art techniques were introduced in Africa.
    (B) Benin sculptures were discovered.
    (C) The Cuban revolution began.
    (D) African art was widely recognized.

47. (A) The British expedition of 1897.
    (B) Cubism.
    (C) Benin carvings.
    (D) Ethnologists.

48. (A) For fifty years.
    (B) Since 1897.
    (C) Since the Cubist period.
    (D) For hundreds of years.

49. (A) As lacking in aesthetic theory.
    (B) As a great art tradition.
    (C) As a shocking discovery.
    (D) As no longer necessary.

50. (A) Bronze castings.
    (B) Benin carvings.
    (C) African masks.
    (D) Cubist works.

THIS IS THE END OF THE LISTENING COMPREHENSION SECTION OF THE TEST

THE NEXT PART OF THE TEST IS SECTION 2. TURN TO THE
DIRECTIONS FOR SECTION 2 IN YOUR TEST BOOK. READ THEM,
AND BEGIN WORK. DO NOT READ OR WORK ON ANY OTHER
SECTION OF THE TEST.

STOP   STOP   STOP   **STOP**   STOP   STOP   STOP

SECTION 2
STRUCTURE AND WRITTEN EXPRESSION
Time: 25 minutes

This section tests your ability to recognize language that is appropriate for standard written English. There are two types of questions in this section, with special directions for each type.

Directions: Questions 1–15 are incomplete sentences. Beneath each sentence, you will see four words or phrases, marked (A), (B), (C), and (D). Choose the *one* word or phrase that best completes the sentence. Then, on your answer sheet, find the number of the question and fill in the space that corresponds to the letter of the answer you have chosen. Fill in the space so that the letter inside the oval cannot be seen.

Example I

Vegetables are an excellent source _____ vitamins.
(A) of
(B) has
(C) where
(D) that

Sample Answer

(● B C D)

The sentence should read, "Vegetables are an excellent source of vitamins." Therefore, you should choose answer (A).

Example II

_____ in history when remarkable progress was made within a relatively short span of time.
(A) Periods
(B) Throughout periods
(C) There have been periods
(D) Periods have been

Sample Answer

The sentence should read, "There have been periods in history when remarkable progress was made within a relatively short span of time." Therefore, you should choose answer (C).

Now begin work on the questions.

GO ON TO THE NEXT PAGE

1. Although we sent out invitations, we have no idea _____ coming to the party.
   (A) who are
   (B) whom are
   (C) who is
   (D) whom is

2. The mayor felt that the police, in spite of the reports, had done _____ best in a difficult situation.
   (A) its
   (B) their
   (C) his
   (D) our

3. The pioneers _____ the frontier had a difficult life with few comforts.
   (A) on
   (B) in
   (C) inside
   (D) over

4. _____ there is a snowstorm or some other bad weather, the mail always comes on time.
   (A) Because
   (B) If
   (C) So
   (D) Unless

5. The typist was fast _____, and was hired immediately.
   (A) but efficient
   (B) and efficiently
   (C) so efficient
   (D) and efficient

6. Since calculators were introduced, they _____ to be useful tools for people weak in math.
   (A) proving
   (B) will prove
   (C) have proved
   (D) are proving

7. The _____ economy at the turn of the century was due in large part to the influx of thousands of immigrants.
   (A) rapid expanding
   (B) rapid expand
   (C) expand rapidly
   (D) rapidly expanding

8. Not being able to determine what _____ is the biggest obstacle for new managers.
   (A) the priority should be
   (B) it should be the priority
   (C) should the priority be
   (D) should be it the priority

9. Mr. Kwok cooks continental cuisine _____ as the best cooks in Europe.
   (A) as good
   (B) as better
   (C) better
   (D) as well

GO ON TO THE NEXT PAGE

10. The nation was founded on the principle that all men are created _____.
    (A) equitable
    (B) equality
    (C) equal
    (D) equilibrium

11. Some doctors involved in brain research _____ that violence has its roots in certain sections of the brain.
    (A) are believing
    (B) believe
    (C) believing
    (D) believes

12. That woman _____ speaking softly can barely be understood.
    (A) whose
    (B) whom is
    (C) who is
    (D) who

13. Even _____ to believe otherwise, the central Arctic is not a solid sheet of ice.
    (A) though many do not want
    (B) many do want not
    (C) though not many do want
    (D) many do not want

14. The language of the Sumerians, _____, is unrelated to any known language.
    (A) which remains obscure origin
    (B) whose origin remains obscure
    (C) whose remains obscure origin
    (D) who is origin obscure remain

15. After _____ the angry mob shouting for his resignation, the President summoned his loyal aids to his office.
    (A) their hearing
    (B) they hearing
    (C) heard
    (D) hearing

GO ON TO THE NEXT PAGE

Directions: In questions 16–40, each sentence has four underlined words or phrases. The four underlined parts of the sentence are marked (A), (B), (C), and (D). Identify the *one* underlined word or phrase that must be changed in order for the sentence to be correct. Then, on your answer sheet, find the number of the question and fill in the space that corresponds to the letter of the answer you have chosen.

Example I

Sample Answer
Ⓐ Ⓑ ● Ⓓ

A ray of light passing <u>through</u> <u>the center</u> of a thin lens <u>keep</u> its <u>original</u> direction.
               A   **B**   **C**   **D**

The sentence should read, "A ray of light passing through the center of a thin lens keeps its original direction." Therefore, you should choose answer (C).

Example II

Sample Answer
Ⓐ Ⓑ Ⓒ ●

The mandolin, a musical <u>instrument</u> <u>that has</u> strings, was probably copied <u>from</u>
                         A   **B**   **C**

the lute, a <u>many</u> older instrument.
      D

The sentence should read, "The mandolin, a musical instrument that has strings, was probably copied from the lute, a much older instrument." Therefore, you should choose answer (D).

Now begin work on the questions.

16. Physics is <u>probably being</u> <u>the most</u> highly <u>organized</u> branch of <u>science</u> today.
                A   **B**   **C**   **D**

17. Psychologists <u>who</u> <u>study</u> sleep habits <u>believes</u> daydreaming <u>is</u> essential.
             A **B**   **C**   **D**

18. People who <u>always</u> on time cannot understand the <u>seemingly</u> intentional
              A   **B**

<u>tardiness</u> of people <u>who</u> are always late.
  C   **D**

GO ON TO THE NEXT PAGE

19. Elizabeth I <u>of England</u> had <u>more wigs</u> in her wardrobe <u>than</u> hairs <u>on their head</u>.
           A   **B**   **C**   **D**

20. Man can <u>control changes</u> <u>in nature by</u> <u>imitating them</u>, by using them, and
             A   **B**   **C**
also <u>man can inhibit</u> them, too.
  D

21. Greek <u>science preserved</u> for <u>posterity</u> by the Arabs, <u>who</u> also introduced the
           A   **B**   **C**
Arabic system <u>of numbers</u>.
     D

22. If <u>a</u> <u>hydrogen-filled</u> balloon is brought <u>near a flame</u>, <u>it exploded</u>.
  A   **B**   **C**   **D**

23. Hormones are chemical <u>substances are produced</u> in the body <u>by structures known</u>
                        A   **B**
<u>as glands, such as</u> sweat <u>glands and</u> salivary glands.
    C   **D**

24. <u>Outside of Japan</u> <u>seldom potters are</u> regarded <u>as</u> anything <u>more than craftsmen</u>.
      A   **B**   **C**   **D**

25. Tourists like <u>to travel</u> to <u>the</u> eastern shore <u>so</u> the food is good, the people are
            A   **B**   **C**
<u>friendly</u>, and the prices are reasonable.
  D

26. <u>Getting used</u> to eating fast food <u>and traffic</u> jams are problems newcomers
      A   **B**
<u>have</u> <u>to</u> face <u>after arriving</u> in Los Angeles.
 C   **D**

27. <u>Today it is</u> almost impossible <u>to imagination</u> the <u>boredom and constrictions</u> of
   A   **B**   **C**
the average middle-class woman's <u>life</u> before World War II.
                    D

GO ON TO THE NEXT PAGE

28. <u>A</u> World Health Organization survey <u>showed that</u> the <u>incidence of eye</u> disease
    A   **B**   **C**

    along <u>the Nile three times</u> that along the Amazon.
          D

29. <u>In a recent ranking</u> of American cities, Rand McNally rated Pittsburgh,
    A

    Pennsylvania, as the most <u>livable</u> city <u>and</u> Yuba City, California, <u>as the less</u>.
                              B   **C**   **D**

30. The <u>hippopotamus kills</u> <u>more men</u> each year <u>than lion</u> and the
        A   **B**   **C**

    <u>elephant combined</u>.
    D

31. The Federal Art Project of 1935 supported some 5,000 <u>artists, enabling</u>
                                                         A

    <u>their to work</u> all over America <u>rather than come</u> to New York <u>in search of a market</u>.
    B   **C**   **D**

32. Six times <u>a day</u> the <u>bell in</u> the tower in <u>the</u> center <u>at the school</u> tolls.
              A   **B**   **C**   **D**

33. <u>Sophisticated</u> <u>communications have</u> taken the challenge <u>out of traveled</u> in
    A   **B**   **C**

    <u>remote</u> places.
    D

34. Since first <u>it being</u> performed <u>on a bare stage</u> <u>in the fifties</u>, Wagner's Ring Cycle
                A   **B**   **C**

    <u>has usually been</u> done in minimalist conceptual decor.
    D

35. <u>Because</u> the African tsetse <u>is a serious threat</u> to human health, <u>it helps</u> maintain
    A   **B**   **C**

    <u>the delicate balance</u> of nature.
    D

GO ON TO THE NEXT PAGE

36. <u>Serious bird watchers</u> must know not only the <u>appearance nor the sounds</u> of the
          A   **B**

    840-odd <u>species that can be</u> counted <u>in North America.</u>
             C   **D**

37. Rhodes Tavern, a quaint building over 200 years old <u>which it will</u> be torn down
                                             A

    soon, <u>was considered</u> a historical monument <u>until</u> investors wanted it.
     B   **C**   **D**

38. Many sociologists <u>believe</u> <u>that sports organized</u> serve <u>both a recreational and</u> a
                   A   **B**   **C**

    social function <u>by reflecting</u> the values of society.
           D

39. Critics of television <u>commercials</u> would prefer <u>that advertisers conform</u> to a
                 A   **B**

    stricter code of ethics <u>than was</u> currently <u>in effect.</u>
             C   **D**

40. <u>Education on</u> environmental issues <u>it should include</u> not only physical
       A   **B**

    <u>problems like pollution</u> but also social <u>problems caused by</u> pollution.
          C   **D**

THIS IS THE END OF SECTION 2

IF YOU FINISH BEFORE TIME IS CALLED, CHECK YOUR WORK
ON SECTION 2 ONLY.
DO NOT READ OR WORK ON ANY OTHER SECTION OF THE TEST. THE
SUPERVISOR WILL TELL YOU WHEN TO BEGIN WORK ON SECTION 3.

SECTION 3
VOCABULARY AND READING COMPREHENSION

Time: 45 minutes

This section tests your comprehension of standard written English. There are two types of questions in this section, with special directions for each type.

Directions: In questions 1–30, each sentence has an underlined word or phrase. Below each sentence are four other words or phrases, marked (A), (B), (C), and (D). You are to choose the *one* word or phrase that *best keeps the meaning* of the original sentence if it is substituted for the underlined word or phrase. Then, on your answer sheet, find the number of the question and fill in the space that matches the letter you have chosen. Fill in the space so that the letter inside the oval cannot be seen.

Example   **Sample Answer**

Passenger ships and <u>aircraft</u> are often equipped with ship-to-   Ⓐ Ⓑ Ⓒ ●
shore air-to-land radio telephones.
(A)   highways
(B)   railroads
(C)   planes
(D)   sailboats
The best answer is (C), because "Passenger ships and planes are often equipped with ship-to-shore or air-to-land radio telephones" is closest in meaning to the original sentence. Therefore, you should choose answer (C).

Now begin work on the questions.

1. The icy roads made driving very <u>hazardous</u>.
   (A)   challenging
   (B)   dangerous
   (C)   slippery
   (D)   exciting

2. After watching the sunset, I was left with a very <u>tranquil</u> feeling.
   (A)   queasy
   (B)   sad
   (C)   peaceful
   (D)   sleepy

3. People with <u>introverted</u> personalities find it difficult to make friends.
   (A)   obnoxious
   (B)   forward
   (C)   reserved
   (D)   outgoing

4. The last mayor was <u>assassinated</u> when he was fifty years old.
   (A)   honored
   (B)   murdered
   (C)   elected
   (D)   impeached

GO ON TO THE NEXT PAGE ➤

5. As a result of the <u>expansion</u> of the public transit system, the university will disband its shuttle bus service.
   (A) problems
   (B) painting
   (C) decrease
   (D) enlargement

6. The child <u>charged</u> down the steps.
   (A) ran
   (B) fell
   (C) tiptoed
   (D) slid

7. The speech was barely <u>audible</u>.
   (A) able to be heard
   (B) able to be read
   (C) able to be understood
   (D) able to be ignored

8. Self-confidence is <u>an essential</u> factor for a successful person.
   (A) a possible
   (B) an integral
   (C) a minor
   (D) a negative

9. The theater critics thought the movie was <u>horrendous</u>, and the audience agreed with them.
   (A) delightful
   (B) dreadful
   (C) spectacular
   (D) obscene

10. The politician's manner was <u>blatantly</u> dishonest, so the election results were not a surprise.
    (A) openly
    (B) hardly
    (C) offensively
    (D) extremely

11. The dog's <u>furtive</u> actions made me worry about him.
    (A) unusual
    (B) sleepy
    (C) secretive
    (D) sickly

12. His <u>audacious</u> behavior shocked his parents.
    (A) daring
    (B) brilliant
    (C) courageous
    (D) quiet

13. The popular singer was as <u>ludicrous</u> in his dress as he was in his speech.
    (A) comical
    (B) loud
    (C) somber
    (D) common

14. The teacher explained the <u>nuances</u> in Frost's poetry to the class.
    (A) images
    (B) subtleties
    (C) rhythm
    (D) rhymes

GO ON TO THE NEXT PAGE

15. The opportune moment had arrived, but few took advantage of it.
    (A) awaited
    (B) lucky
    (C) appropriate
    (D) anticipated

16. The travel agent tried to tantalize me with details of a proposed trip to the islands.
    (A) tempt
    (B) dissuade
    (C) inform
    (D) fool

17. The natural elements obliterated the writing from the walls of the monument.
    (A) outlined
    (B) erased
    (C) covered
    (D) produced

18. The sealed chambers of the ancient pharaohs were the goal of the expedition.
    (A) hidden
    (B) unreachable
    (C) ancient
    (D) closed

19. Many of the pictures were reproduced and enlarged.
    (A) taken again
    (B) printed again
    (C) renewed
    (D) restored

20. The valley, wild and inaccessible, had been the haunt of bandits.
    (A) unreachable
    (B) desolate
    (C) high
    (D) dry

21. Children often imitate their parents.
    (A) copy
    (B) criticize
    (C) admire
    (D) remember

22. The administration took for granted that we would agree.
    (A) hoped
    (B) assumed
    (C) guaranteed
    (D) were convinced

23. The tenor's singing captivated the audience.
    (A) frightened
    (B) bored
    (C) disgusted
    (D) enchanted

24. A review of the history of economics shows a recession may precede a depression.
    (A) point to
    (B) come before
    (C) indicate
    (D) cause

GO ON TO THE NEXT PAGE

25. The punishment should reflect the severity of the crime.
    (A) seriousness
    (B) purpose
    (C) location
    (D) perpetrator

26. Many animals collect a supply of food for the winter.
    (A) bury
    (B) desire
    (C) accumulate
    (D) require

27. The robot, although reliable, has limited use.
    (A) dependable
    (B) automatic
    (C) versatile
    (D) fast

28. In the United States, a typical work day is eight hours long.
    (A) characteristic
    (B) complete
    (C) total
    (D) hard

29. If you are visiting a foreign country, you may be unaccustomed to eating unfamiliar foods.
    (A) surprised at
    (B) unused to
    (C) disappointed in
    (D) afraid of

30. Because the teenager was ashamed that she failed her driving test, she would not come home.
    (A) disappointed
    (B) unhappy
    (C) humiliated
    (D) disgusted

GO ON TO THE NEXT PAGE

Directions: In the rest of this section you will read several passages. Each one is followed by several questions about it. For questions 31–60, you are to choose the *one* best answer, (A), (B), (C), or (D), to each question. Then, on your answer sheet, find the number of the question and fill in the space that matches the letter of the answer you have chosen.

Answer all questions following a passage on the basis of what is *stated* or *implied* in the reading passage.

Example passage and questions

The rattles with which a rattlesnake warns of its presence are formed by loosely interlocking hollow rings of hard skin, which make a buzzing sound when its tail is shaken. As a baby, the snake begins to form its rattles from the button at the very tip of its tail. Thereafter, each time it sheds its skin, a new ring is formed. Popular belief holds that a snake's age can be told by counting the rings, but this idea is fallacious. In fact, a snake may lose its old skin as often as four times a year. Also, rattles tend to wear or break off with time.

Example I

A rattlesnake's rattles are made of

(A) skin
(B) bone
(C) wood
(D) muscle

Sample Answer
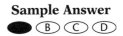

According to the passage, a rattlesnake's rattles are made of rings of hard skin. Therefore, you should choose answer (A).

Example II

How often does a rattlesnake shed its skin?

(A) Once every four years
(B) Once every four months
(C) Up to four times every year
(D) Four times more often than other snakes

Sample Answer
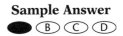

The passage states that "a snake may lose its old skin as often as four times a year." Therefore, you should choose answer (C).

Now begin work on the questions.

GO ON TO THE NEXT PAGE

Questions 31–35

Some of the properties of magnets were known from very early times. For example, it was known over 2,000 years ago that the mineral magnetite, an oxide of iron, possesses the property of attracting iron. The Chinese, earlier than 2,500 B.C., knew that if a piece of magnetite is suspended so that it can turn freely in a horizontal plane it will set in a definite direction and can therefore be used as a primitive compass. Later it was found that if a bar of iron is rubbed with a piece of magnetite, or lodestone, the magnetic properties of the lodestone are transferred to the iron. The lodestone is called a natural magnet, as distinct from other types of magnets, which are made by various artificial processes.

Magnets today are usually made of special alloys of steel. A steel magnet differs from ordinary steel and from all other substances in three important respects: It attracts iron filings, it sets in a definite direction when freely suspended, and it converts iron and steel bars in its neighborhood into magnets. If we place a bar magnet in iron filings it will emerge with a cluster of filings attached to each end, showing that there is a center of magnetic force at each end of the bar. These centers are called the poles of the magnet. A bar magnet suspended horizontally in a paper stirrup will always set with the line joining its poles along a north and south line; in other words, the magnet has a north-seeking pole and a south-seeking pole. A bar magnet floating on a cork will set roughly north and south but it will not move either to the north or to the south, showing that the two poles are equal in strength. If we bring the north pole of one magnet close to the south pole of another magnet, the unlike poles attract one another, but if we bring two north poles or two south poles into proximity we find that like poles repel one another.

31. In what way are most modern magnets different from ancient ones?
    (A) They attract iron filings.
    (B) They set in a definite direction.
    (C) They are artificial.
    (D) They convert iron into magnets.

32. The ancient Chinese are known to have used magnets to
    (A) attract iron filings
    (B) make steel alloys
    (C) float corks
    (D) indicate direction

GO ON TO THE NEXT PAGE

33. According to the passage, how
    many magnetic centers are there in
    each bar magnet?
    (A) 1
    (B) 2
    (C) 3
    (D) 4

34. Which of the following is the best
    title for the passage?
    (A) Varieties of Magnets
    (B) How Magnets Work
    (C) The History of the Magnet
    (D) The Many Uses of Magnets

35. In this passage, the writer makes
    repeated use of
    (A) argumentative language
    (B) examples
    (C) technical terminology
    (D) hypothesis

GO ON TO THE NEXT PAGE

Questions 36–41

The study of business planning has a long history. For example, in 1916 in one of the earliest efforts to develop a science of management, Henri Fayol discussed the importance of planning for successful management and described the development of one-year and five-year budget plans. In his book he gives the following definition
5 of business planning:

"The maxim managing means looking ahead' gives some idea of the importance attached to planning in the business world, and it is true that if foresight is not the whole of management, at least it is an essential part of it. To foresee, in this context, means both to assess the future and make provisions for it. . . . The plan of action is,
10 at one and the same time, the result envisaged, the line of action to be followed, the stages to go through and methods to use."

Subsequent studies of general management written during the next fifty years echo Fayol's thinking and reveal both a continuing interest in the subject and an ever-increasing awareness of how important planning is to successful business
15 management. In their definitions of the planning process, the authors of these studies all stress two important aspects of planning: assessing the future and making plans to deal with the future.

36. Which of the following statements expresses the main idea of the passage?
   (A) Foresight is critical in business planning.
   (B) Know your methods.
   (C) A science of management needs to be developed.
   (D) The results of management studies from the past fifty years have changed dramatically.

37. It can be inferred from the passage that
   (A) Henri Fayol was not looking ahead when he wrote his book
   (B) five-year budget plans are preferable to one-year plans
   (C) interest in assessing the future has only recently been considered important in business planning
   (D) few studies regarding business planning were done prior to 1916

GO ON TO THE NEXT PAGE

38. In line 8, the phrase "an essential part of it" refers to
    (A) foresight
    (B) management
    (C) the future
    (D) study

39. In line 8, the phrase "in this context" means
    (A) according to the dictionary
    (B) as usual
    (C) as is used here
    (D) in the future

40. Writers on management working after Fayol have generally
    (A) reinforced Fayol's ideas
    (B) emphasized budgets instead of time
    (C) evolved away from Fayol's future orientation
    (D) questioned the value of long-term planning

41. This passage covers management studies for the years
    (A) 1900–1966
    (B) 1916–1950
    (C) 1916–1966
    (D) 1916–present

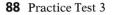

GO ON TO THE NEXT PAGE

Questions 42–47

When early versions of the typewriter first appeared on the market 100 years ago, salesmen loved the arrangement of letters on the keyboard because they could write TYPEWRITER without leaving the top row. At the time, it impressed customers. It hasn't since.

After a century of typos, back strain and repetitive motion injuries, the standard QWERTY keyboard—so named for the first six letters of the third row—is considered one of the true abominations of modern design. Of the ten letters, ADEHINORST, for example, which make up about 70 percent of English words, just three are on the middle keys where the fingers normally rest. One of the ten requires the right index finger to jump to the left, six require the hands to hurdle a row either up or down, and one of the alphabet's most commonly used letters, A, is struck by the pinky, the weakest finger.

In recent years, customer complaints about QWERTY have led to a number of suggestions for improving the keyboard. Instead of rearranging the keys to minimize hand movement, as proposed unsuccessfully in the past, a number of researchers would junk the conventional keyboard in favor of much smaller arrays in which the typist would play combinations or chords of keys, much like a piano.

One of the most recent and ambitious chording arrangements, developed by Virginia engineer Larry Langley with the help of the Navy, has just eight keys, one for each finger. Each key has two active positions, front and back, which gives the typist a total of 64 combinations, corresponding to all letters of the alphabet and other necessary keyboard functions.

42. Which of the following statements best expresses the author's opinion of the standard typewriter keyboard?
    (A) It is the optimal arrangement for speed typing.
    (B) It is an exemplary example of modern design.
    (C) It was not designed well.
    (D) The keys need to be rearranged to minimize hand movement.

43. Which of the following does the author mention as a cause for changing the keyboard?
    (A) the suggestions of researchers
    (B) the advice of typewriter salespeople
    (C) customer complaints
    (D) new technology

GO ON TO THE NEXT PAGE

44. The passage suggests an answer to which of the following questions?
    (A) Why do only ten letters make up about 70 percent of English words?
    (B) Has anyone designed a successful keyboard arrangement?
    (C) How can typists avoid typographical errors?
    (D) When will new chording arrangements be available to the public?

45. How does the author organize the discussion of typewriter keyboards?
    (A) The author gives the background and outlines a number of suggestions.
    (B) The author states the problem, and supports his opinion with numerous examples.
    (C) The author gives the history, the subsequent problems, and one solution.
    (D) The author offers a rationale for his suggestions.

46. What is the author's attitude toward revised keyboard arrangements?
    (A) guarded
    (B) enthusiastic
    (C) hopeful
    (D) critical

47. In the first paragraph, the word "it" refers to
    (A) the arrangement of letters
    (B) early versions of the typewriter
    (C) typewriter salesmen
    (D) the first typewriter

GO ON TO THE NEXT PAGE

Questions 48–53

The idea for the founding of Tucson was brought forth on a hot day in August 1775, when a colonel in the Spanish army, Don Hugo Oconor, and one of the greatest missionaries in the history of the Spanish expansion in the New World, Father Francisco Garces, decided that a military outpost was needed at a small settlement
5 along the Santa Cruz River.

The outpost was to be a part of the Spanish system of presidios, or garrisons, of which there were seventeen along a 2,000-mile frontier stretching through what is now Texas, New Mexico, northern Mexico, Arizona, and California. The existence of the presidios served a dual purpose for the Spanish—to protect their interests from
10 marauding Indians and, later, to form the genesis of new communities. The place along the river the men chose had been settled much earlier by ancestors of the local Pima Indians. The name *Tucson* is a Spanish corruption of the Pima word meaning "the place at the foot of the black mountain."

In June of 1777, a new commander, Captain Don Pedro Allande, was assigned to
15 the fledgling presidio. When Spanish government funds were not available to build fortifications at the renamed San Augustin del Tucson, the money came from Captain Allande. On May Day 1782, the presidio was attacked by a force of 600 Apaches. The garrison survived, but Captain Allande was convinced that further protection was needed. He pushed for the completion of a three-foot-thick adobe
20 wall ten to twelve feet high to enclose San Augustin del Tucson.

48. What does the passage mainly discuss?
   (A) The military strategy of Captain Don Pedro Allande
   (B) The history of the origin of Tucson
   (C) The beginnings of presidios
   (D) The importance of Indians in the founding of Tucson

49. It can be concluded from the passage that
   (A) Tucson is located at the base of a mountain.
   (B) Spanish is the most common language in the area.
   (C) the communities are very religious.
   (D) Tucson was originally settled by the Mexicans.

GO ON TO THE NEXT PAGE

50. The author implies that Don Pedro Allande was
    (A) a Pima Indian
    (B) a poor commander
    (C) a missionary
    (D) a rich man

51. According to the passage, Tucson was founded as
    (A) a mission
    (B) a military outpost
    (C) an Indian reservation
    (D) the seat of the government

52. The paragraph following the passage most probably discusses
    (A) the layout of the city
    (B) instances of Indian attacks
    (C) a description of how the wall was built
    (D) the remaining six presidios

53. In line 12, the word "corruption" most probably means
    (A) destruction
    (B) breakage
    (C) translation
    (D) implication

GO ON TO THE NEXT PAGE

Questions 54–60

How vividly most people remember the experience of being read to as children! They can tell you exactly whether it was mother or dad who read at bedtime. They know it was Aunt Louise who specialized in Kipling, and Mrs. Rossi in third grade who read *Charlotte's Web* the last thing every afternoon.

A loved adult's voice conjures up a colorful story-world. The memory evokes such warm and contented feelings as recollections of infant nursing might hold, if we could remember back that far. Indeed, the two experiences have common elements: the physical and emotional closeness of adult and child, the adult's attentiveness to the child, and the aim of satisfying a hunger. Clearly, both activities are nurturing ones.

But is the disappearance of communal reading something to mourn? Perhaps it's just a case of having replaced one pleasant pastime with others—gathering around the television set for "Monday Night Football," for instance. Maybe it balances out.

But no. We all recognize that the loss is a real loss, not just a change, and that the shared pleasure of reading aloud is not the only casualty. Many children today grow up with negative attitudes toward books and reading in any form. The media call it "a literacy crisis." The schools try new methods of teaching reading and test children more often, but nothing seems to cure the problems. Publishers bring out attractive books geared to poor readers; teachers report that these students are so turned off by books that the new formats don't entice them at all. Worried parents invest in expensive "teach your child to read" kits and high-powered electronic learning games, only to see their children growing up reading nothing on their own but an occasional comic book.

Meanwhile, research data have slowly been accumulating that suggest how we might resolve this crisis. Several studies of children from widely varied backgrounds who learned to read easily and remained good readers throughout their school years have revealed that they had something in common. They all had been read to regularly from early childhood and had as models adults or older children who read for pleasure.

54. What does the passage mainly discuss?
    (A) Recollections of communal reading
    (B) The value of reading aloud
    (C) New methods of teaching reading
    (D) Resolving negative attitudes about reading

55. Which of the following does the author mention as a possible cause for the decrease in communal reading?
    (A) Computer games
    (B) Television
    (C) Overscheduled children
    (D) Exhausted parents

GO ON TO THE NEXT PAGE

56. According to the passage, what do good readers have in common?
    (A) They had library cards and were able to find high-interest books.
    (B) They were read to often as children and saw others reading for pleasure.
    (C) Their parents guided them through "teach your child to read" kits and computer games.
    (D) They attended schools with new methods of teaching reading.

57. The passage supports which of the following conclusions?
    (A) Parents play a critical role in their children's education.
    (B) Television viewing should be banned during the school year.
    (C) The benefits of communal TV watching can be comparable to communal reading.
    (D) The literacy crisis will worsen in the near future.

58. To which of the following activities does the author compare being read to?
    (A) Watching television
    (B) Nursing as an infant
    (C) Playing video games
    (D) Modeling reading opportunities

59. What does the paragraph following the passage most probably discuss?
    (A) Types of books that lend themselves to reading aloud
    (B) Additional explanations of the results of the research
    (C) Warnings about limiting communal reading
    (D) Reasons why children have negative attitudes toward reading

60. Which of the following best describes the tone of the passage?
    (A) Comical and realistic
    (B) Neutral but serious
    (C) Relaxed but persuasive
    (D) Arrogant and scathing

THIS IS THE END OF SECTION 3

IF YOU FINISH BEFORE TIME IS CALLED, CHECK YOUR WORK
ON SECTION 3 ONLY.
DO NOT READ OR WORK ON ANY OTHER SECTION OF THE TEST.

PRACTICE TEST 4

SECTION 1
LISTENING COMPREHENSION

The questions in Section 1 of the test are on a recording.

In this section of the test, you will have an opportunity to demonstrate your ability to understand spoken English. There are three parts to this section, with special directions for each part.

Part A

Directions: For each question in Part A, you will hear a short sentence. Each sentence will be spoken just one time. The sentence you hear will not be written out for you. Therefore, you must listen carefully to understand what the speaker says.

After you hear a sentence, read the four choices in your test book, marked (A), (B), (C), and (D), and decide which *one* is closest in meaning to the sentence you heard. Then, on your answer sheet, find the number of the question and fill in the space that matches the letter of the answer you have chosen. Fill in the space so that the letter inside the oval cannot be seen.

Example I   **Sample Answer**
   You will hear: *Mary swam out to the island with her friends.*   Ⓐ Ⓑ ● Ⓓ
   You will read: (A) Mary outswam the others.
                    (B) Mary ought to swim with them.
                    (C) Mary and her friends swam to the island.
                    (D) Mary's friends owned the island.

The speaker said, "Mary swam out to the island with her friends." Sentence (C), "Mary and her friends swam to the island," is closest in meaning to the sentence you heard. Therefore, you should choose answer (C).

Example II   **Sample Answer**
   You will hear: *Would you mind helping me with this load*   Ⓐ ● Ⓒ Ⓓ
                   of books?
   You will read: (A) Please remind me to read this book.
                    (B) Could you help me carry these books?
                    (C) I don't mind if you help me.
                    (D) Do you have a heavy course load?

The speaker said, "Would you mind helping me with this load of books?" Sentence (B), "Could you help me carry these books?" is closest in meaning to the sentence you heard. Therefore, you should choose answer (B).

GO ON TO THE NEXT PAGE

1. (A) I couldn't hear well.
   (B) The bugs ran through the dust.
   (C) I got dusty beating the rug.
   (D) My hair is clean.

2. (A) Two boys completed the course.
   (B) Nine boys took the entire course.
   (C) Eleven boys didn't want to finish.
   (D) Thirteen boys wouldn't take the course.

3. (A) There were 17 reservations.
   (B) There were 17 of us.
   (C) Thirty-two people came to the party.
   (D) The party was on the 15th.

4. (A) Many people know who he was.
   (B) Nobody paid any attention.
   (C) He became infamous.
   (D) He had no good intentions.

5. (A) He has never studied geology.
   (B) The geologist had never seen a cannon.
   (C) The canyon was not unique.
   (D) The geologist was impressed.

6. (A) The trainer must return all sports equipment.
   (B) The school no longer is in session.
   (C) All school equipment is used for sports.
   (D) The trainer is in charge of the school's equipment.

7. (A) Nobody could find paper clips.
   (B) We could clip the hedges.
   (C) The eclipse was invisible.
   (D) People went outside to get a good view.

8. (A) The fireman yelled, "Fire!"
   (B) We called them to put out the fire.
   (C) You put out the fire when you were called.
   (D) The fire burned because no one was there to put it out.

9. (A) Jim saw the movie before I did.
   (B) I saw the movie before Jim.
   (C) I saw the movie, then ate.
   (D) Jim ate, then saw the movie.

10. (A) Plan C is the most comprehensive.
    (B) Plan A is better than Plan C.
    (C) Plan B is less complete than Plan A.
    (D) Plan A is less comprehensive than Plan C.

11. (A) The further the distance, the narrower the river.
    (B) Her wide smile is contagious.
    (C) You can see her smile from here.
    (D) The river gets wider a few miles away.

GO ON TO THE NEXT PAGE

12. (A) The bus started after the bags were loaded.
    (B) Two of us pulled the candy away from the boys.
    (C) The suitcases were left on the curb.
    (D) Those attending brought a bag lunch.

13. (A) She always stays away from hospitals.
    (B) The county erected a memorial to the wounded.
    (C) Many people don't value their vote.
    (D) Some ballots were not counted.

14. (A) The beds are in a long row in the room.
    (B) The batteries are dead.
    (C) Photographers work long hours.
    (D) The film was overexposed.

15. (A) The technicians were reluctant to work.
    (B) The technicians deserve more responsibility.
    (C) The technician did not earn our trust.
    (D) The technician worked without pay.

16. (A) They avoided the problem by obeying the rules.
    (B) The rules were not followed.
    (C) Ignoring the rules caused no problem.
    (D) They were unaware of the rules.

17. (A) The program finished sooner than expected.
    (B) The series of programs was very long.
    (C) The issue grew worse over time.
    (D) These problems are hardly serious.

18. (A) The Board reviewed 13 committees.
    (B) The committee recommended 30 items.
    (C) The review took half an hour.
    (D) The Board refused to consider the recommendations.

19. (A) We were not on time.
    (B) The ceremony began 30 minutes ago.
    (C) We'll leave within the next 30 minutes.
    (D) We're going to be tardy.

20. (A) The sun shone after the rain.
    (B) Rye is a shiny grain.
    (C) I would have polished it.
    (D) The wood had a gray color.

GO ON TO THE NEXT PAGE

Part B

Directions: In Part B you will hear short conversations between two speakers. At the end of each conversation, a third person will ask a question about what was said. You will hear each conversation and question about it just one time. The sentence you hear will not be written out for you. Therefore, you must listen carefully to understand what the speaker says. After you hear a conversation and the question about it, read the four possible answers in your test book and decide which *one* is the best answer to the question you heard. Then, on your answer sheet, find the number of the question and fill in the space that matches the letter of the answer you have chosen.

Example   **Sample Answers**
   You will hear:
      (first man)   *Professor Smith is going to retire soon. What*
                        kind of gift shall we give her?
        (woman)   *I think she'd like to have a photograph of our class.*
   (second man)   *What does the woman think the class should do?*
   You will read: (A) Present Professor Smith with a picture.
                        (B) Photograph Professor Smith.
                        (C) Put glass over the photograph.
                        (D) Replace the broken headlight.

From the conversation you learn that the woman thinks Professor Smith would like a photograph of the class. The best answer to the question "What does the woman think the class should do?" is (A), "Present Professor Smith with a picture." Therefore, you should choose answer (A).

21. (A) The woman should walk faster.
    (B) The woman is a fast walker.
    (C) The woman can't walk.
    (D) The woman walks too quickly.

22. (A) Met friends.
    (B) Saw a movie.
    (C) Went for a walk.
    (D) Made a phone call.

23. (A) The man can't drive.
    (B) The party is over.
    (C) They can't turn around.
    (D) They're lost.

24. (A) A librarian.
    (B) A laborer.
    (C) A banker.
    (D) A thief.

25. (A) Her grandfather's.
    (B) Her mother's.
    (C) Her brother's.
    (D) Her father's.

26. (A) A hand.
    (B) His briefcase.
    (C) A typewriter.
    (D) His papers.

GO ON TO THE NEXT PAGE

27. (A) Look for work.
    (B) Take a lonely cruise.
    (C) Buy a horse.
    (D) Cut the grass.

28. (A) 7
    (B) 8
    (C) 18
    (D) 80

29. (A) 50 cents.
    (B) $1.00.
    (C) $1.50.
    (D) $2.00.

30. (A) The shirts.
    (B) The color.
    (C) The size.
    (D) The suits.

31. (A) Look for his friends.
    (B) Go outside.
    (C) Stay inside.
    (D) Take a train.

32. (A) She started swimming.
    (B) She stopped reading.
    (C) She baked some bread.
    (D) She lost weight.

33. (A) At a park.
    (B) In a classroom.
    (C) At an office.
    (D) At church.

34. (A) She's not hungry.
    (B) She'd prefer to cook.
    (C) She wants to go out.
    (D) She only wants to sleep.

35. (A) There will be inflation.
    (B) Prices should increase.
    (C) She shouldn't have to diet.
    (D) She should lose weight.

GO ON TO THE NEXT PAGE

Part C

Directions: In this part of the test, you will hear short talks and conversations. After each of them, you will be asked some questions. You will hear the talks and conversations just one time. They will not be written out for you. Therefore, you must listen carefully in order to understand what the speaker says.

After you hear a question, read the four possible answers in your test book and decide which *one* is the best answer to the question you heard. Then, on your answer sheet, find the number of the question and fill in the space that matches the letter of the answer you have chosen.

Answer all questions on the basis of what is *stated* or *implied* in the talk or conversation.

Listen to this sample talk.
You will hear:
(first man)   *Balloons have been used for about a hundred years. There are two kinds of sport balloons, gas and hot air. Hot-air balloons are safer than gas balloons, which may catch fire. Hot-air balloons are preferred by most balloonists in the United States because of their safety. They are also cheaper and easier to manage than gas balloons. Despite the ease of operating a balloon, pilots must watch the weather carefully. Sport balloon flights are best early in the morning or late in the afternoon, when the wind is light.*

Now look at the following example.   **Sample Answers**
You will hear: Ⓐ ● Ⓒ Ⓓ
(second man)   *Why are gas balloons considered dangerous?*
You will read: (A) They are impossible to guide.
                     (B) They may go up in flames.
                     (C) They tend to leak gas.
                     (D) They are cheaply made.

The best answer to the question "Why are gas balloons considered dangerous?" is (B), "They may go up in flames." Therefore, you should choose answer (B).

GO ON TO THE NEXT PAGE

Now look at the next example.
  You will hear:
  (second man) *According to the speaker, what must balloon pilots be careful to do?*
  You will read: (A) Watch for changes in weather.
                     (B) Watch their altitude.
                     (C) Check for weak spots in their balloons.
                     (D) Test the strength of the ropes.

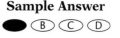

  The best answer to the question "According to the speaker, what must balloon pilots be careful to do?" is (A), "Watch for changes in weather." Therefore, you should choose answer (A).

36. (A) People are either intelligent or not.
    (B) Humans have multiple intelligences.
    (C) IQs are not indicative of intelligence.
    (D) People are born without intelligence.

37. (A) IQs are extremely important.
    (B) Secrets must be uncovered.
    (C) All people are smart.
    (D) People can be both smart and stupid.

38. (A) Superior cultures.
    (B) Different abilities.
    (C) Intelligence quotients.
    (D) Intelligent races.

39. (A) Minimal.
    (B) None whatsoever.
    (C) Essential.
    (D) Inexplicable.

40. (A) We're smart in different ways.
    (B) Some are smarter than others.
    (C) They are discovered.
    (D) Their IQs reflect their intelligences.

41. (A) Undesirable.
    (B) Necessary.
    (C) Fattening.
    (D) Damaging.

42. (A) Calories.
    (B) Proteins.
    (C) Cereal.
    (D) Energy.

43. (A) Hamburgers.
    (B) Fruit salad.
    (C) Ice cream.
    (D) Purified water.

44. (A) Cereal grains.
    (B) Animals.
    (C) Plants.
    (D) Vegetables.

GO ON TO THE NEXT PAGE

45. (A) Oxygen.
    (B) Plant tissue.
    (C) Proteins.
    (D) Carbon.

46. (A) California.
    (B) New York.
    (C) Pennsylvania.
    (D) Mississippi.

47. (A) A strong back.
    (B) A lot of money.
    (C) A promise of gold.
    (D) A permit.

48. (A) The prospectors.
    (B) The merchants.
    (C) The cattle ranchers.
    (D) The mule herder.

49. (A) A wife.
    (B) Strong sons.
    (C) A mule.
    (D) Good hands.

50. (A) They're uninhabited.
    (B) They now have zoos.
    (C) Gold has made them
        prosperous.
    (D) They are full of merchants.

THIS IS THE END OF THE LISTENING COMPREHENSION SECTION OF THE TEST

THE NEXT PART OF THE TEST IS SECTION 2. TURN TO THE
DIRECTIONS FOR SECTION 2 IN YOUR TEST BOOK. READ THEM,
AND BEGIN WORK. DO NOT READ OR WORK ON ANY OTHER
SECTION OF THE TEST.

SECTION 2
STRUCTURE AND WRITTEN EXPRESSION
Time: 25 minutes

This section tests your ability to recognize language that is appropriate for standard written English. There are two types of questions in this section, with special directions for each type.

Directions: Questions 1–15 are incomplete sentences. Beneath each sentence, you will see four words or phrases, marked (A), (B), (C), and (D). Choose the *one* word or phrase that best completes the sentence. Then, on your answer sheet, find the number of the question and fill in the space that corresponds to the letter of the answer you have chosen. Fill in the space so that the letter inside the oval cannot be seen.

Example I

Vegetables are an excellent source _____ vitamins.

Sample Answer

(A) of
(B) has
(C) where
(D) that

The sentence should read, "Vegetables are an excellent source of vitamins." Therefore, you should choose answer (A).

Example II

_____ in history when remarkable progress was made within a relatively short span of time.

Sample Answer

(A) Periods
(B) Throughout periods
(C) There have been periods
(D) Periods have been

The sentence should read, "There have been periods in history when remarkable progress was made within a relatively short span of time." Therefore, you should choose answer (C).

Now begin work on the questions.

1. Powder when mixed with water
   _____.
   (A) dissolving
   (B) dissolves
   (C) dissolve
   (D) is dissolve

2. _____ is thought to be one of the best investments of the decade.
   (A) That the artist works
   (B) The artist's works
   (C) The work of that artist
   (D) That the artist's work

3. Water boils _____ if there is a cover on the pan.
   (A) faster
   (B) more fast
   (C) as fast as
   (D) most fast

4. In one year rats eat 40 to 50 times _____ weight.
   (A) its
   (B) and
   (C) their
   (D) of

5. If there were life on Mars, such life forms _____ unable to survive on Earth.
   (A) would be
   (B) are
   (C) will be
   (D) would

6. Little is known about platinum _____ so little of it exists.
   (A) but
   (B) why
   (C) because
   (D) although

7. The damage was caused by either the earthquake _____ the subsequent explosions.
   (A) and
   (B) but
   (C) then
   (D) or

8. After _____, the supernova hurls its mass into the black void of space.
   (A) explode
   (B) exploding
   (C) explosive
   (D) explodes

9. Severe reactions to bee stings among adults _____ than once believed.
   (A) more are probably common
   (B) more common probably are
   (C) are more probably common
   (D) are probably more common

GO ON TO THE NEXT PAGE

10. The vineyards are open all year
    except for August, which _____.
    (A) the best time to harvest is
    (B) is the best time to harvest
    (C) to harvest is the best time
    (D) the best time is to harvest

11. Because of intermittent charging by
    the _____, the lights flickered.
    (A) generating
    (B) generation
    (C) generator
    (D) generated

12. New research in geophysics
    disproved _____ had been a
    universally accepted truth.
    (A) that
    (B) which
    (C) whom
    (D) what

13. The static interference on the radio
    _____ an airplane.
    (A) was caused by
    (B) was causing
    (C) has caused
    (D) caused by

14. Water vapor _____ on a window
    pane produces condensation.
    (A) which accumulating
    (B) accumulating
    (C) accumulates
    (D) is accumulating

15. The management requests that all
    personnel _____ their complaints
    to their immediate supervisor.
    (A) will direct
    (B) directs
    (C) directing
    (D) direct

GO ON TO THE NEXT PAGE

Directions: In questions 16–40, each sentence has four underlined words or phrases. The four underlined parts of the sentence are marked (A), (B), (C), and (D). Identify the *one* underlined word or phrase that must be changed in order for the sentence to be correct. Then, on your answer sheet, find the number of the question and fill in the space that corresponds to the letter of the answer you have chosen.

Example I

Sample Answer
Ⓐ Ⓑ ● Ⓓ

A ray of light passing <u>through</u> <u>the center</u> of a thin lens <u>keep</u> its <u>original</u> direction.
                 A   **B**   **C**   **D**

The sentence should read, "A ray of light passing through the center of a thin lens keeps its original direction." Therefore, you should choose answer (C).

Example II

Sample Answer
Ⓐ Ⓑ Ⓒ ●

The mandolin, a musical <u>instrument</u> <u>that has</u> strings, was probably copied <u>from</u>
                    A   **B**   **C**

the lute, a <u>many</u> older instrument.
        D

The sentence should read, "The mandolin, a musical instrument that has strings, was probably copied from the lute, a much older instrument." Therefore, you should choose answer (D).

Now begin work on the questions.

16. Because of <u>the rising cost</u> of living, more families today <u>they are</u> discovering
                  A   **B**

     that <u>both husband and</u> wife <u>must work</u>.
          C   **D**

17. A team <u>of specialists</u> <u>concluded that</u> the <u>patient's blindness</u> was <u>contemporary</u>.
              A   **B**   **C**   **D**

GO ON TO THE NEXT PAGE

18. <u>After given</u> the award, <u>the recipient of</u> the Peace Prize made a short acceptance
       A   **B**

speech, <u>which was followed</u> by a <u>standing ovation</u>.
              C   **D**

19. When <u>the Spanish</u> constructed <u>its missions</u> <u>in the New World</u>, they incorporated
            A   **B**   **C**

<u>Moorish architectural features</u>.
       D

20. Marcel Duchamp, who died <u>in</u> 1969, <u>is known</u> <u>as</u> the artist who <u>has abandoned</u>
                                A   **B**   **C**   **D**

art for chess.

21. <u>Although the country's</u> military <u>budget</u> is insufficient, the army <u>be expected</u>
            A   **B**   **C**

<u>to perform well</u> in war.
       D

22. <u>After</u> two weeks of intensive computer training, the new recruits <u>were allowed</u>
    A   **B**

to <u>write a program</u> <u>theirselves</u>.
       C   **D**

23. <u>The archaeologist</u> believed <u>which the tomb</u> <u>discovered in</u> North Africa
            A   **B**   **C**

<u>belonged to</u> one of Hannibal's generals.
       D

24. Meteorologists <u>have been using</u> both computers <u>or</u> satellites <u>to help make</u>
    A   **B**   **C**

     weather forecasts <u>for</u> two decades.
                 D

25. <u>There is</u> a folk myth that <u>an horsehair</u> <u>in</u> a container of rainwater placed in the
    A   **B**   **C**

     sunshine <u>will develop</u> into a snake.
               D

26. <u>The Arctic</u> ice pack is 40 <u>percent thin</u> and 12 percent smaller <u>in area</u> than it was
    A   **B**   **C**

     <u>a half</u> a century ago.
        D

27. Crime prevention <u>experts believe</u> that if the <u>possession</u> of <u>small firearms</u> were
                A   **B**   **C**

     limited, crime and <u>violence decreased</u>.
                   D

28. <u>For nesting and shelter</u>, the sparrow <u>seeks out</u> the seclusion <u>and being secure</u>
            A   **B**   **C**

     offered by tangled vines and <u>thick bushes</u>.
                    D

29. <u>The advent</u> of calculators <u>did fundamentally</u> changed <u>the teaching methods</u>
    A   **B**   **C**

     for <u>mathematics</u>.
         D

30. Aluminum, <u>which making</u> up about 8 percent of <u>the Earth's</u> crust, <u>is</u>
              A   **B**   **C**

     <u>the most abundant</u> metal available.
             D

GO ON TO THE NEXT PAGE

31. The screenwriter <u>who provides</u> the words <u>for a film</u> <u>is acclaimed seldom</u>, unlike
              A   **B**   **C**

    the director and the <u>actors and actresses</u>.
                       D

32. The cowboy epitomizes the belief <u>held by</u> many Americans <u>for rugged</u>
                            A   **B**

    <u>individualism</u> and <u>the frontier spirit</u>.
       C   **D**

33. <u>Most early</u> immigrants <u>are coming</u> from an <u>agricultural</u> background found work
     A   **B**   **C**

    on farms.
     D

34. <u>Recently</u> gasoline manufacturers have begun to develop <u>additives will reduce</u>
     A   **B**

    the <u>harmful</u> emissions <u>from automobile engines</u>.
         C   **D**

35. <u>People, when</u> they sleep <u>less than</u> normal, <u>awake</u> more friendly and
        A   **B**   **C**

    more aggression.
       D

36. <u>As cooling</u> slows <u>the life</u> process, blood cells in the laboratory <u>is stored</u> at
      A   **B**   **C**

    low temperatures.
       D

GO ON TO THE NEXT PAGE

37. The lawyers <u>for the administration</u> <u>met</u> with the representative of the
      A   **B**

 <u>students had been</u> occupying the building for <u>a week</u>.
   C   **D**

38. Restaurant patrons <u>who stay</u> after 11 o'clock will not <u>be able</u> to use <u>public</u>
      A   **B**   **C**

 transportation to <u>have returned</u> home.
      D

39. The citizens, <u>who been</u> tolerant <u>of the mayor's</u> unsavory practices in the past,
     A   **B**

 <u>finally impeached</u> the <u>amoral politician</u>.
   C   **D**

40. <u>During</u> the Industrial Revolution, the <u>birth rate</u> in Europe <u>declined</u>,
 A   **B**   **C**

 <u>as the death rate</u>.
   D

THIS IS THE END OF SECTION 2

IF YOU FINISH BEFORE TIME IS CALLED, CHECK YOUR WORK
ON SECTION 2 ONLY.
DO NOT READ OR WORK ON ANY OTHER SECTION OF THE TEST. THE
SUPERVISOR WILL TELL YOU WHEN TO BEGIN WORK ON SECTION 3.

SECTION 3
VOCABULARY AND READING COMPREHENSION

Time: 45 minutes

This section tests your comprehension of standard written English. There are two types of questions in this section, with special directions for each type.

Directions: In questions 1–30, each sentence has an underlined word or phrase. Below each sentence are four other words or phrases, marked (A), (B), (C), and (D). You are to choose the *one* word or phrase that *best keeps the meaning* of the original sentence if it is substituted for the underlined word or phrase. Then, on your answer sheet, find the number of the question and fill in the space that matches the letter you have chosen. Fill in the space so that the letter inside the oval cannot be seen.

Example

Passenger ships and <u>aircraft</u> are often equipped with ship-to-shore or air-to-land radio telephones.
(A) highways
(B) railroads
(C) planes
(D) sailboats

Sample Answers

(A) (B) ● (D)

The best answer is (C), because "Passenger ships and planes are often equipped with ship-to-shore or air-to-land radio telephones" is closest in meaning to the original sentence. Therefore, you should choose answer (C).

Now begin work on the questions.

1. The <u>issue</u> we are discussing concerns everyone who has children.
   (A) subject
   (B) book
   (C) article
   (D) equation

2. The evaluation stated that the secretary's work has been <u>satisfactory</u>.
   (A) whimsical
   (B) adequate
   (C) audacious
   (D) comprehensive

GO ON TO THE NEXT PAGE

3. The hospital is looking for people willing to <u>donate</u> their organs.
   (A) sell
   (B) retrieve
   (C) give
   (D) show

4. Most teenagers think their actions are <u>mature</u>.
   (A) grown-up
   (B) intelligent
   (C) serious
   (D) childlike

5. The chorale wanted to <u>rehearse</u> the song before the performance.
   (A) delete
   (B) rewrite
   (C) introduce
   (D) practice

6. After an extended break, the class <u>resumed</u>.
   (A) continued
   (B) returned
   (C) repeated
   (D) receded

7. Prejudice <u>toward</u> minorities probably stems from fear of the unknown.
   (A) concerning
   (B) upon
   (C) through
   (D) around

8. The bank needed some <u>assurance</u> that the loan would be repaid.
   (A) contract
   (B) approval
   (C) guarantee
   (D) presence

9. The sign requested that we <u>extinguish</u> all fires before leaving the campground.
   (A) count
   (B) put out
   (C) remember
   (D) locate

10. Invitations were <u>extended</u> to everyone who had worked on the project.
    (A) offered to
    (B) mandated for
    (C) shown to
    (D) intended for

11. The roof of the house was <u>practically</u> falling in and the front steps were rotting away.
    (A) almost
    (B) obviously
    (C) always
    (D) conveniently

12. Their <u>inept</u> handling of our account made us reevaluate our relationship with them.
    (A) dishonest
    (B) clever
    (C) clumsy
    (D) competent

13. The article <u>alluded to</u> the devastation in the countryside, caused by the wind storms.
    (A) misrepresented
    (B) referred to
    (C) forgot about
    (D) recounted

GO ON TO THE NEXT PAGE

14. The zealous demonstrators were ignored by the media.
    (A) ardent
    (B) colorful
    (C) rude
    (D) clever

15. No one ever knew the reason for the enmity between the two families.
    (A) relationship
    (B) hatred
    (C) friendship
    (D) remoteness

16. The teacher thought the aspiring writer's essays were verbose.
    (A) interesting
    (B) concise
    (C) clever
    (D) redundant

17. The organizer's intransigent manner helped her get her way.
    (A) honest
    (B) stubborn
    (C) friendly
    (D) loud

18. The humidity made us more lethargic than usual.
    (A) thirsty
    (B) slow
    (C) warm
    (D) careless

19. People usually think cats are naturally ferocious, but it depends on the type of cat.
    (A) friendly
    (B) furry
    (C) savage
    (D) independent

20. Generosity is believed to be an innate quality of man.
    (A) a hidden
    (B) a benevolent
    (C) a natural
    (D) an unselfish

21. The greatest physical distinction between humans and apes is the hollow space humans have under their chins.
    (A) attraction
    (B) danger
    (C) comfort
    (D) difference

22. Physicists have made discoveries that challenge our most fundamental theories of the universe.
    (A) basic
    (B) permanent
    (C) interesting
    (D) ancient

23. The most recent research indicates that dinosaurs were warm-blooded animals.
    (A) disputes
    (B) insists
    (C) suggests
    (D) disproves

24. Contrary to popular belief, Cleopatra, the famous Egyptian queen, was Greek, spoke six languages, and was a brilliant military strategist.
    (A) an intelligent
    (B) a known
    (C) a professional
    (D) a popular

GO ON TO THE NEXT PAGE

25. An archaeologist must know <u>exactly</u> where and when an artifact was found.
    (A) intuitively
    (B) immediately
    (C) briefly
    (D) precisely

26. The budget director wanted to <u>be certain that</u> his officers were aware of the deadline.
    (A) ask if
    (B) pretend that
    (C) make sure that
    (D) know if

27. The cab driver was <u>discourteous</u>.
    (A) handsome
    (B) rude
    (C) irritable
    (D) lost

28. The children in the neighborhood have a club that <u>excludes</u> everyone over eight.
    (A) laughs at
    (B) avoids
    (C) leaves out
    (D) invites

29. What is the <u>gist</u> of the article?
    (A) ending
    (B) length
    (C) title
    (D) point

30. A good magician can make an elephant <u>disappear</u>.
    (A) behave
    (B) forget
    (C) learn
    (D) vanish

GO ON TO THE NEXT PAGE

Directions: In the rest of this section you will read several passages. Each one is followed by several questions about it. For questions 31–60, you are to choose the *one* best answer, (A), (B), (C), or (D), to each question. Then, on your answer sheet, find the number of the question and fill in the space that matches the letter of the answer you have chosen.

Answer all questions following a passage on the basis of what is *stated* or *implied* in the reading passage.

Example passage and questions

The rattles with which a rattlesnake warns of its presence are formed by loosely interlocking hollow rings of hard skin, which make a buzzing sound when its tail is shaken. As a baby, the snake begins to form its rattles from the button at the very tip of its tail. Thereafter, each time it sheds its skin, a new ring is formed. Popular belief holds that a snake's age can be told by counting the rings, but this idea is fallacious. In fact, a snake may lose its old skin as often as four times a year. Also, rattles tend to wear or break off with time.

Example I

A rattlesnake's rattles are made of

(A) skin
(B) bone
(C) wood
(D) muscle

Sample Answer

● Ⓑ Ⓒ Ⓓ

According to the passage, a rattlesnake's rattles are made of rings of hard skin. Therefore, you should choose answer (A).

Example II

How often does a rattlesnake shed its skin?

(A) Once every four years
(B) Once every four months
(C) Up to four times every year
(D) Four times more often than other snakes

Sample Answer

Ⓐ Ⓑ ● Ⓓ

The passage states that "a snake may lose its old skin as often as four times a year." Therefore, you should choose answer (C).

Now begin work on the questions.

GO ON TO THE NEXT PAGE

Questions 31–37

The names that admiring naturalists have given to hummingbirds suggest exquisite, fairylike grace and gemlike refulgence. Fiery-tailed awlbill, ruby-topaz hummingbird, glittering-bellied emerald—these are a few of the colorful names that I find applied to some of the 233 species of hummingbirds briefly described in Meyer
5 de Schauenesee's *Guide to the Birds of South America.*

One would expect one's first glimpse of a creature that bears one of these glamorous names to be a breathtaking vision of beauty. Often the birdwatcher is disappointed. To behold the hummingbird's most vivid colors, he or she may have to wait patiently before flowers that it habitually visits, until it turns squarely toward
10 the viewer. Then the gorget or the crown—usually the male hummingbird's most glittering part—which at first appeared to be lusterless, suddenly gleams with the most intense metallic green, blue, violet, magenta, or ruby, like a sunbeam suddenly breaking through a dark cloud. The fiery glitter is often all too brief, for with the first turn of the hummer's body it expires as suddenly as it flared up. How different from
15 the bright colors of such birds as tanagers, orioles, and wood warblers, which are visible at a glance and show to almost equal advantage from any angle.

31. Which of the following does the author mainly discuss?
    (A) Birds of South America
    (B) Hummingbirds
    (C) Tanagers, orioles, and wood warblers
    (D) Colors

32. According to the passage, which statement is true?
    (A) Hummingbirds are visible at a great distance.
    (B) Hummingbirds are found only in South America.
    (C) It's difficult to see the beautiful colors of hummingbirds.
    (D) Male hummingbirds are lusterless.

GO ON TO THE NEXT PAGE

33. Which of the following does the author imply?
    (A) Orioles and hummingbirds have similar colors.
    (B) The male hummingbird is more colorful than the female.
    (C) There are only a few different types of hummingbirds.
    (D) Hummingbirds show their beautiful colors from every angle.

34. The words "he or she" (line 8) refer to
    (A) the hummingbird
    (B) Meyer de Schauenesee
    (C) a bird watcher
    (D) the author

35. The tone of the passage could best be described as
    (A) objective
    (B) reverential
    (C) critical
    (D) dismissive

36. The author compares the hummingbird with tanagers, orioles, and wood warblers because
    (A) they are colorful
    (B) they like flowers
    (C) they are frequently seen
    (D) they move quickly

37. What does the word "it" in line 14 refer to?
    (A) the fiery glitter
    (B) the first turn
    (C) a sunbeam
    (D) the hummer's body

GO ON TO THE NEXT PAGE

Questions 38–43

At the worker level, technology can affect the social relationships among people by bringing about changes in such human elements as the size and composition of the work group or the frequency of contact with other workers. E. L. Trist and K. W. Bamforth discovered this when they conducted research among post-World War I
5 coal miners. The miners initially worked in small, independent, cohesive groups. However, advances in technology and equipment led to changes in the composition of these work groups, and the result was a decline in productivity. Only when management restored many of the social and small-group relationships did output again increase.
10 It is perhaps the greatest fear of workers faced with new technology that the machinery will lead to the abolition of jobs or to the reduction of tasks to such simplistic levels that workers can hardly endure the stress of their new, extremely dull functions. Since the human being must be able to support one or more persons by means of work and since the mind resists its own belittling, such changes,
15 brought about by advancing technology, have a profound effect on the psychosocial system. In order to prevent intolerable upheaval, management must be simultaneously and equally aware of the social (human) and the technical (operational) aspects and needs of the organization.

38. What is the main idea of the passage?
    (A) Small groups work more efficiently than large ones.
    (B) Modern work methods are inhumane and degrading.
    (C) Efficiency in the workplace results from a balance of social and technological factors.
    (D) The technology of mining is constantly evolving.

39. The author's purpose in the passage is to
    (A) urge workers to form unions
    (B) suggest ways to prevent disruption in the workplace
    (C) argue for smaller work groups
    (D) discourage rapid technological change in the workplace

GO ON TO THE NEXT PAGE

40. Which of the following best describes the author's attitude toward the workers?
    (A) Puzzled
    (B) Critical
    (C) Interested
    (D) Supportive

41. The author uses the word "output" (line 8) in the passage to mean
    (A) tasks
    (B) productivity
    (C) increase
    (D) advances

42. At which point does the author begin to discuss supporting evidence?
    (A) Line 1
    (B) Line 3
    (C) Line 8
    (D) Line 10

43. The paragraph immediately following the passage probably discusses
    (A) details about post-World War I miners
    (B) how workers support their families
    (C) details about social aspects and needs in the workplace
    (D) how to resist change in the workplace

GO ON TO THE NEXT PAGE

Questions 44–50

Hospitals and surgery can be especially frightening for children, and to help lessen young patients' anxiety, one drug company has been experimenting with sedative "lollipops." Recently the U.S. Food and Drug Administration (FDA) gave the go-ahead to further testing of sweet-tasting fentanyl suckers on children, despite protests from a consumer health group that the lollipop form will give kids the idea that drugs are candy. Fentanyl, a widely used narcotic anesthetic agent, is 200 times more potent than morphine.

Fentanyl lollipops can ease kids' separation from their parents and make the administration of anesthesia go more smoothly, according to a member of the team that tested them. But the Public Citizen Health Research Group, alarmed by what it believes is a danger to children and a new opportunity for drug abuse, urged the FDA to call a halt to the experiments. Fentanyl is so addictive, according to the group's director, Dr. Sidney Wolfe, that its widespread availability could cause drug-abuse problems. He suggests that hospitals develop other ways to calm young patients, such as making greater use of play therapy and allowing parents to accompany children into the operating room.

Dr. Gary Henderson, a pharmacologist and an authority on fentanyl abuse, doubts that carefully controlled use of the drug in a hospital setting would pose a danger or suggest to kids that drugs are like candy. "Children will associate few things in the hospital with a pleasant experience," he says.

44. Which of the following is the best title for the passage?
    (A) Children's Fears
    (B) Play Therapy versus Fentanyl
    (C) Dangerous Medicines for Children
    (D) Narcotic Lollipops

45. According to the passage, why does the Public Citizen Health Research Group protest the use of fentanyl lollipops?
    (A) Testing for effectiveness has not been completed.
    (B) Fentanyl is addictive, and could therefore be abused.
    (C) The lollipops contain too much sugar, and could possibly affect the teeth of the children.
    (D) Morphine is preferable for sedating children.

GO ON TO THE NEXT PAGE

46. According to the passage, what advantage do the lollipops have over regular anesthesia?
    (A) They are easier to administer.
    (B) They are less costly.
    (C) They are more potent.
    (D) They are safer.

47. Which of the following is NOT mentioned as a way of lessening young patients' anxieties regarding surgery?
    (A) Sedative lollipops
    (B) Play therapy
    (C) Parents' presence in the operating room
    (D) Children's books about anesthesia

48. The passage supports which of the following conclusions?
    (A) Fentanyl lollipops have been declared safe for children.
    (B) Sedative lollipops have caused children to have no fears regarding surgery.
    (C) The use of sedative lollipops is controversial.
    (D) Medical doctors agree that fentanyl lollipops will be considered beneficial in the future.

49. Which of the following words best describes the tone of the passage?
    (A) Critical
    (B) Didactic
    (C) Informative
    (D) Insistent

50. The author uses the quote in the last sentence to indicate
    (A) that children are usually optimistic about hospital stays
    (B) there is always something memorable about hospitals
    (C) that young patients can be taught to enjoy hospitals
    (D) that children don't usually enjoy hospital stays

GO ON TO THE NEXT PAGE

Questions 51–56

What issues are of concern to today's teenagers? How do they view themselves and the world in which they live? How do they rate their schools in terms of helping them prepare for adulthood? These were the basic questions answered by the 1988 American Home Economics Association's Survey of American Teenagers. Interviews with 510 high school juniors and seniors, selected to represent the U.S. high school population by sex and by race/ethnicity, indicated that the world of today's teenagers is a balance of positive and negative influences.

Teenagers identified issues relating to money, the future, and health as ones that worry them most. At least three in ten were "extremely" or "very" concerned about being able to pay for college, not earning enough money, making the wrong decisions about their futures, contracting AIDS, and the future of the United States. Issues relating to career choice, marriage, family financial well-being, combining work and family responsibilities, dealing with family crises, and nutrition and disease were of concern to at least one in five surveyed.

Further, teenagers reported that the schools are doing only an "adequate" job of teaching them the skills necessary for a responsible and productive life. Schools received the highest ratings in life-skill areas related to health concerns (substance abuse, human sexuality, and AIDS), choosing a career, and making important life decisions. But teenagers perceived that they were least prepared by schools in matters related to family life/parenting, choosing a marital partner, and dealing with family crises, such as death and divorce.

51. With which topic is the passage mainly concerned?
    (A) American teenagers' preparation for adulthood
    (B) Results of a survey of American teenagers
    (C) Positive and negative influences on American teenagers
    (D) Current home economics curricula

52. According to the passage, which of the following is considered one of the most worrisome issues facing teenagers today?
    (A) A decrease in academic skills
    (B) Racial problems
    (C) Future financial problems
    (D) The high rate of divorce

GO ON TO THE NEXT PAGE

53. According to the passage, which of the following is NOT mentioned as an area in which schools are sufficiently preparing their teenagers?
   (A) Health
   (B) Careers
   (C) Drugs
   (D) Academics

54. It can be inferred from the passage that
   (A) the students surveyed were chosen for their academic abilities
   (B) those surveyed were from various parts of the United States
   (C) most of the students surveyed were in vocational studies
   (D) the teenagers surveyed were enrolled in home economics classes

55. With which of the following statements would the author of the passage be LEAST likely to agree?
   (A) Today's American teenagers are mostly pessimistic about their future.
   (B) American teenagers are satisfied with their educational programs.
   (C) The results of the survey reflect the consensus of most American teenagers.
   (D) American teenagers are somewhat dissatisfied with the current family life education programs available in their high schools.

56. The paragraph following the passage most probably discusses
   (A) the likelihood of increasing the number of academic course requirements
   (B) the need for additional funding for health-related courses
   (C) how the survey was administered and how the results were calculated
   (D) program improvement and curriculum in life-skills programs

GO ON TO THE NEXT PAGE

Questions 57–60

Stories are often told about telephone operators from all over the United States getting inquiries about foreign long-distance rates to New Mexico. The post office in Albuquerque receives U.S. mail affixed with international airmail stamps. The occasional first-time visitor will bring a passport. Although it has been a part of the U.S. since 1912, New Mexico's 122,000 square miles can seem like a foreign country to those unfamiliar with it. More than any other state, it has held on to—and nurtured—its historic roots. Spanish flows easily from the lips of residents. Native Americans still live in ancient cities built by their forebears and participate in age-old traditions.

Yet New Mexico, which has a history and culture traceable for thousands of years, is perhaps the most "American" of all the states; it could be said that it is the cradle of this country's civilization. Long before European feet trod on Plymouth Rock, they left footprints in New Mexico.

Although the presence of man in New Mexico can be traced back more than 25,000 years, it is generally thought that today's Pueblo Indians are descendants of the Anasazi, a culture that flourished from before the birth of Christ to the thirteenth century. The Anasazi and their descendants were mostly peaceful people, agrarian and social, who lived together in small villages.

57. What is the main topic of this passage?
    (A) The Anasazi way of life
    (B) The geography of the Southwest
    (C) A history of New Mexico
    (D) Various Native American tribes

58. According to the passage, when did man first appear in New Mexico?
    (A) About 25,000 years ago
    (B) At around the thirteenth century
    (C) At the time of the arrival of Europeans
    (D) Since 1912

59. The author implies, but does not state, that
    (A) the Anasazi preceded the Pueblo Indians
    (B) New Mexico is one of the largest states in the U.S.
    (C) many people consider New Mexico part of Mexico
    (D) the Anasazi were farmers

60. In the first paragraph, the phrase "Native Americans" could best be replaced by which of the following?
    (A) The Anasazi
    (B) Pueblo Indians
    (C) New Mexicans
    (D) Albuquerque residents

THIS IS THE END OF SECTION 3

DO NOT READ OR WORK ON ANY OTHER SECTION OF THE TEST.

STOP   STOP   STOP   **STOP**   STOP   STOP   STOP

APPENDIX

❏ PRACTICE TEST TAPESCRIPTS

PRACTICE TEST 1

PART A

1. (Man A) Joan will fly rather than drive.
2. (Man B) Swimming is better exercise than walking.
3. (Woman) Raise your hand if you don't understand.
4. (Man B) The morning weather report follows the local news.
5. (Man B) Margaret's directions are so simple anyone can follow them.
6. (Man A) Mary saw two movies in one afternoon.
7. (Man B) Mark was the last one off the bus.
8. (Woman) Don't work so much.
9. (Man A) Why don't we have lunch one of these days?
10. (Woman) When we moved to this city, we made many new friends.
11. (Man B) Since the weather was warm, we waited outside.
12. (Woman) If you're going past the post office, I need some stamps.
13. (Man B) I'm sorry, but I'll be late tomorrow.
14. (Man A) To get a gym locker, you have to sign up in the Athletic Office.
15. (Woman) Do you prefer classical music to rock?
16. (Man B) If you mail the letter this afternoon, they should receive it next Monday.
17. (Woman) The library is open until six tonight, but it is closed tomorrow.
18. (Man A) Since the light is not very good in this room, could you turn on another light?
19. (Man B) You should read the directions before starting the experiment.
20. (Man A) I must finish this book by the end of the week.

PART B

21. (Man A) I'd like to apply for a loan, please.
    (Woman) Fill out this form and see one of our officers.
    (Man B) Where are they?
22. (Woman) I finally have an appointment with my doctor.
    (Man B) You've had that cold all week, haven't you?
    (Man A) What can we assume about the woman?
23. (Man B) I've been here for 25 minutes. How often do the buses pass here?
    (Woman) They usually come every 15 minutes.
    (Man A) Where does this conversation probably take place?
24. (Man B) I think I'll make some tea. Would you like some?
    (Woman) Yes, please. Is there any cream or sugar?
    (Man A) What will the man probably do?
25. (Woman) The classrooms are usually cleaned twice a week, on Monday and Wednesday.
    (Man A) Well, let's have them done on Friday, too.
    (Man B) How often will the classrooms be cleaned from now on?
26. (Man A) Every time I call the number, I get a busy signal.
    (Woman) Wait an hour and try again.
    (Man B) What does the woman suggest the man do?
27. (Woman) Are we going to eat at 5 or 6?
    (Man B) We'll eat at 4 because the movie starts at 6:30.

(Man A)	What are they going to do first?	
28. (Woman)	I'm sorry, sir. This section of the restaurant is for nonsmokers.	
(Man B)	I thought this WAS the smoking section.	
(Man A)	Why is the man upset?	
29. (Man A)	We'd better hurry. I'm afraid we'll miss the plane.	
(Woman)	Relax. We've got plenty of time. Have some more coffee.	
(Man B)	How does the man feel?	
30. (Man A)	Can you read this card for me?	
(Man B)	You forgot your glasses again, didn't you?	
(Woman)	What does the conversation mean?	
31. (Man B)	You can't park your car here. This is a school entrance.	
(Woman)	I'll only be a minute, officer.	
(Man A)	What does the woman want to do?	
32. (Woman)	How soon until you retire?	
(Man A)	Well, I'll be 65 next week, and I'll walk out that door then.	
(Man B)	What will the man do next week?	
33. (Woman)	Fill it up and check the oil, please.	
(Man B)	Could you pull a little closer to the pump, please?	
(Man A)	Where does this conversation probably take place?	
34. (Man B)	I hope you'll be able to join us for lunch tomorrow.	
(Woman)	I'd like to, but I'm meeting a friend at the train station.	
(Man A)	What does the woman mean?	
35. (Man B)	I didn't make a reservation. Do you have a room for tonight?	
(Woman)	I'm sorry. We're completely booked.	
(Man A)	Where does this conversation probably take place?	

PART C

(Man A) Questions 36 through 41 refer to the following lecture.

(Woman) Dreams have always interested poets and philosophers, but in the last decade scientists became interested in dreams, too. What is the meaning of dreams? What is their purpose? It seems that our dreams at night affect our mood during the day. Scientists have determined that our feelings of happiness or unhappiness may depend on our dreams.

By observing people sleeping, scientists have concluded that normal sleep is divided into 5 distinct stages: stages 1 through 4 and REM. REM is an acronym for rapid eye movement. Most dreaming takes place during REM and, for most adults, REM occurs four to six times a night.

What we dream at night is not as important as whom we dream about. More precisely, the number of people in our dreams is the important element. The more people in our dreams, the happier we will be. Conversely, the fewer people in our dreams, the less happy we will be.

Psychiatrist Milton Kramer believes that "the bad thing in a dream is to be alone." There is something about interacting with people that produces happiness both in our dreams and when we are awake.

36. (Man B)	What has always interested poets and philosophers?
37. (Man B)	When did scientists become interested in dreams?
38. (Man B)	How many stages of sleep are there?
39. (Man B)	What does the "R" in REM stand for?
40. (Man B)	What do people usually experience during REM?
41. (Man B)	What is the effect of interacting with many people in a dream?
(Man A)	Questions 42 through 45 refer to the following dialog.
(Woman)	I wish that girl would turn down her music. I can't stand this noise. I think I'm going to go deaf.

(Man B) Well, you might! Noise is a serious health hazard. I read that if we're exposed to over 100 decibels for two hours or more we can suffer hearing loss.

(Woman) How much is that? I'm sure that kid with her stereo must be over 100.

(Man B) Close to it. Amplified music is only about 95 decibels, but a rock concert is about 130. Teenagers and people in their twenties are going to suffer hcaring loss without a doubt. Noise is harmful for other reasons, too. If a noise wakes us up in the middle of the night, we experience stress. Stress is a factor in a variety of health problems, from heart disease to high blood pressure.

(Woman) There must be some local ordinances that prohibit excessive noise. I'll check into it, but if people want to hurt their eardrums, it's their business. Still, I want to hear the birds sing when I get older.

42. (Man A) What are the speakers concerned about?

43. (Man A) After how many hours of exposure to high-decibel noise does it become harmful?

44. (Man A) Which group is likely to experience the most impaired hearing?

45. (Man A) About how many decibels is a rock concert?

(Man B) Questions 46 through 50 refer to the following lecture.

(Man A) As part of your first assignment for the introductory course to archaeology, I want you all to collect a bag of garbage from different neighborhoods and analyze it.

You may think this sounds funny, but that's exactly what archaeologists do: study ancient garbage. We look at the bones, the pot shards, and even the refuse around the fire to make guesses about the socioeconomic status of the inhabitants of a given area.

In this class, we will make the same kinds of assumptions, except we will use garbage from our lifetime—"contemporary garbage."

Our students last semester searched through bags of half-empty jars of food, bottles, wrappers, vegetable peels—everything that people would throw away. They discovered that middle-income households buy more lamb, pork, and chicken, and surprisingly, throw bits of it away. This group tended to waste food. On the other hand, both poor and wealthy families bought better-quality food and wasted less of it. Another interesting and unpredictable fact was that lower-income households bought expensive educational toys and kitchen materials.

By studying the garbage patterns of our neighborhoods, we will be able to validate last semester's hypotheses or challenge them. And that's what scientific investigation is about— making a hypothesis, testing it, and revising it. Now go collect that garbage.

46. (Woman) When was this lecture probably given?

47. (Woman) What class was the lecture given in?

48. (Woman) What is said about middle-income families?

49. (Woman) Which item would a lower-income household probably NOT buy?

50. (Woman) Why are the students collecting garbage?

PRACTICE TEST 2

PART A

1. (Woman) How did you get here?
2. (Man B) I haven't received my newspaper for two days.
3. (Man A) The exam will be on the first four chapters of the book.
4. (Man B) If you are hungry, why don't you have a snack?
5. (Woman) The taxi cost us ten dollars from the airport to the town.
6. (Man B) How about taking a ride this afternoon?
7. (Man A) I have too much homework to go out this weekend.
8. (Woman) The train was supposed to be here ten minutes ago.
9. (Man A) I woke up when the phone rang.
10. (Woman) These parking spaces are reserved for faculty and visitors.
11. (Man B) Did Richard return the books to the library yet?
12. (Man A) When you see the statue, you'll turn right and go two more blocks.
13. (Woman) We can count on over 2,000 people to come to the conference this weekend.
14. (Man A) I always watch the 6 p.m. news on Channel 4.
15. (Man B) My phone's been out of order since last week.
16. (Woman) The fire broke out on the building's third floor.
17. (Man B) Mr. Johnson went to bed at 10, but didn't fall asleep until midnight.
18. (Man A) Let's get something to eat before the movie.
19. (Woman) My grades aren't good enough to get into the best schools.
20. (Man B) The grass on our lawn will die unless we get some rain.

PART B

21. (Woman) Was Mrs. Smith the first to arrive this morning?
    (Man A) Yes, but she forgot to turn on the air conditioning.
    (Man B) What does the man imply?
22. (Man A) For tomorrow's test, can we use a calculator?
    (Man B) No, you should learn basic calculation skills.
    (Woman) What subject are they talking about?
23. (Man B) Do you know where my glasses are? I thought I left them on the bookshelf.
    (Woman) I saw them on top of your briefcase on the hall table.
    (Man A) What did the man lose?
24. (Man B) Do you want to read this book when I'm finished?
    (Woman) I'd like to, but I don't have time.
    (Man A) What does the woman imply?
25. (Man B) Good afternoon, May I help you?
    (Man A) Yes, I want to mail this package and buy some stamps.
    (Woman) Where is this conversation taking place?
26. (Man A) Another rejection letter! I'll never get into a good school.
    (Woman) Maybe you should take a year off and travel.
    (Man B) Why is this man so upset?
27. (Woman) Is this the check-cashing line?
    (Man A) Yes, and also the line for deposits and withdrawals.
    (Man B) Where is this conversation probably taking place?
28. (Woman) How do you take your coffee? Milk? Sugar?
    (Man B) Actually, I would prefer tea, if it's not too much trouble.
    (Man A) What does this man mean?
29. (Man B) We're out of paper. I'll run and get some.
    (Man A) I'll go with you. I can use some air.
    (Woman) Where will they probably go?
30. (Man B) Congratulations. You earned that grade.
    (Woman) I really studied for that exam. Now, I can take it easy for a while.
    (Man A) Why is the woman so happy?

31. (Woman) Have you written your paper yet? It's due tomorrow morning.
    (Man A) No, I plan to stay up all night.
    (Man B) What does the man imply?
32. (Woman) Help me move this desk over by the window, would you?
    (Man B) The last time I helped you move something, my back hurt for a week.
    (Man A) Why does the woman want help?
33. (Man A) Would you like a one-way or round-trip ticket?
    (Woman) I'm coming back by car, so one-way is all I need.
    (Man B) What is the woman about to do?
34. (Woman) I'm going to make my weekly visit to Mary tonight.
    (Man B) She's been in the hospital for a month, hasn't she?
    (Man A) How long has Mary been sick?
35. (Man A) You need exact change or a token for the bus.
    (Woman) Guess I'll have to take a cab.
    (Man B) What does the woman mean?

PART C

(Man B) Questions 36 through 40 refer to the following dialog.
(Man A) This month is the anniversary of the Moon Walk.
(Woman) You're not talking about the dance, I presume.
(Man A) No, in 1969, Neil Armstrong and Buzz Aldrin stepped on the moon.
(Woman) I was just kidding. How could I forget that? I was teaching an introduction to geology class for majors at the University of Colorado. We were glued to the television set. Then, when the astronauts returned, specimens of the lunar surface were sent to certain schools. We were able to keep several moon rocks in our science museum.
(Man A) Did the rocks look different from the average rock you see on the side of the road?

(Woman) In appearance, not particularly, but there are differences in composition. One of the more interesting differences is that moon rocks lack water. Also, the moon rocks contain oxygen, but not the kind of oxygen earth rocks have. For example, the oxygen in moon rocks can be released through heating.
There are two simple classifications of moon rocks—light rocks and dark rocks. The dark rocks come from what we call the lowland areas of the moon. These areas were impacted by a meteor or meteorite, and consequently the rocks are very dense—fused together like lava.
Light rocks, on the other hand, come from highland areas and are less dense.
(Man A) Are there any places on earth that have similar rocks?
(Woman) Well, a few places. Rocks like the basalts and breccia [note pronunciation brecchia] are found in Iceland, Hawaii, and the western part of the United States.
(Man A) I wonder if we'll ever be mining the minerals on the moon.
36. (Man B) What distinguishes moon rocks from those on earth?
37. (Man B) How does oxygen in moon rocks differ from that in earth rocks?
38. (Man B) Where were the darker rocks found?
39. (Man B) What caused the impacted lowland areas of the moon?
40. (Man B) According to the passage, where on Earth can rocks similar to moon rocks be found?
(Woman) Questions 41 through 45 refer to the following lecture.
(Man A) In a private-enterprise economy, it is common, ordinary people like you and me that determine what goods

are produced and what services are provided. If we are not willing to buy a particular brand of car, or a particular color of a car, that car or that color car will go out of production. If we find that we need someplace to put our children while we work, we create a demand—in this case, a demand for day care centers for children.

It is the demand or lack of demand that determines what restaurants will open and stay open, what products will line the shelves and what ones will be taken off. You can notice, when you look at magazines from the forties or fifties, how advertisements have changed.

Magazines of the forties glorify train travel as fast, comfortable, and even elegant. No travel ads today can legitimately push elegance, but trains continue to push comfort and convenience. New technology, for example, jet planes, has caused us to change our demand.

Our demand can change because our own tastes change. (We may prefer to slow down and take the train; this will cause a demand for improved train service.) Or demand may change because our income changes. (In this case, we purchase our own railroad car.)

These three factors—our tastes, our income, and new technologies—influence demand. But notice that as demand for one product decreases, demand for another product will increase. If a car is too expensive, we will take the bus, or walk. This increases the demand for good walking shoes.

41. (Man B) Who is responsible for the availability of goods and services?

42. (Man B) Why would more red cars be produced than white?

43. (Man B) Who created a demand for day care centers?

44. (Man B) What caused the demise of train travel?

45. (Man B) What factor will cause improved train service?

(Man B) <u>Questions 46 through 50</u> refer to the following dialog.

(Man A) I'm going to an exhibition of photographs this afternoon. Would you like to come?

(Woman) That depends. Who's the photographer?

(Man A) It's a group show. No one famous *yet.*

(Woman) "Yet" is an important word. Photography is becoming a very popular art form. Gallery owners will really try to promote young photographers to make sure their prices go up and up.

(Man A) You know you can buy photographs from the middle of the nineteenth century cheaper than you can buy some contemporary work.

(Woman) Well, price doesn't always equal quality. Fads and fashion dictate price, not quality. It's hard to determine what is art, isn't it? Some of the photographs look just like snapshots, others are very stylized. But even the photographs that look as informal as snapshots take a long time to set up and shoot.

(Man A) Quality art can be determined by what a museum buys and exhibits. If a museum buys an artist, his work becomes more valuable. I don't like to buy art if I can't resell it at a good price. I have to like the piece, of course, but I want to make sure I can resell it later at a higher price than I bought it.

46. (Man B) How was photography defined?
47. (Man B) What could be said about contemporary photographs in relation to older photographs?
48. (Man B) Which, according to the man, is the determiner of quality?
49. (Man B) What word characterizes snapshots?
50. (Man B) How does the man determine what to buy?

PRACTICE TEST 3

PART A

1. (Man A) The plane flew west over the mountains from Denver to Utah.
2. (Man B) We've been trying to call since 11:00, and it's 11:30 now.
3. (Woman) The woman tore her dress when she sat down.
4. (Man A) The exam would not have been as easy if I hadn't studied.
5. (Man B) The flight from Brazil was listed to arrive at 6:10, but by 7:00 it still hadn't arrived.
6. (Woman) The magazine was sent to the printer before it was approved by the editor.
7. (Man A) We threw a blanket over our shoulders to protect us from the sudden downpour.
8. (Man B) The anger he displayed showed he would not listen to reason.
9. (Woman) I have never heard a story about orphans that didn't make me want to weep.
10. (Man A) Prizes were given to all employees who had been with the company for at least five years.
11. (Man B) The grain embargo was only one of the bills occupying the senator's attention.
12. (Woman) The strong gusts caused the speaker to hold onto his papers.
13. (Man A) I rose at 8:30 to make my 9 o'clock class, but I was still 15 minutes late.
14. (Man B) Unless electric consumption is reduced, the city will have to triple its power generation capacity by next year.
15. (Woman) If there had been greater support, the motion would have been approved.
16. (Man A) The commander gave the enlisted men their awards, promoting two to a higher rank.
17. (Man B) The shuttle mission could have lasted longer had the pump not malfunctioned.
18. (Woman) The display monitor showed that a typing error occurred.
19. (Man A) The gas tank in my new car is larger than the one in my old car, but gas was less expensive for my old car than it is now.
20. (Man B) We went to bed at midnight, but we set the alarm to wake us early at 5:00.

PART B

21. (Woman) I'm going to the doctor. I have something wrong with my contact lenses.
    (Man A) That's too bad.
    (Man B) What does the man mean?
22. (Woman) Do you get up at 5 every morning?
    (Man A) Yes, and I need seven hours of sleep. I should go to bed by 9 or 10, I guess.
    (Man B) How much sleep does the man need?
23. (Woman) The 5:00 bus is more expensive but faster.
    (Man A) To save 80 cents, I'll wait 20 minutes for the 5:20.
    (Man B) What bus will the man take?

24. (Man A)   I'm exhausted today. I can't work anymore.
    (Woman)   We still have to finish the report for tomorrow's deadline.
    (Man B)   What describes the man?
25. (Man A)   If you hadn't mentioned their dinner party, I could have gone home.
    (Woman)   That would have been the third time you've disappointed them this month.
    (Man B)   What's he going to do?
26. (Man A)   Mrs. Smith, have you, or your husband, or any members of your family suffered from any form of mental illness?
    (Woman)   No, but my father's family has a history of heart problems.
    (Man B)   Who suffers from heart disease?
27. (Woman)   I could be ready sooner if you'd help me take out the trash.
    (Man A)   Sure. Where do I take it?
    (Man B)   What does the woman want?
28. (Woman)   Be glad you aren't at the other restaurant. They serve even bigger meals.
    (Man A)   This is more than I can eat. Even you can't finish it all.
    (Man B)   What does the man mean?
29. (Man A)   After I take my car to be repaired, I'll go straight to my office.
    (Woman)   Please stop for groceries on the way home if you have time.
    (Man B)   What will the man do first?
30. (Woman)   My shoes are too new. I even wore thick socks and I got blisters.
    (Man A)   Perhaps you walked too far. You should wear new shoes only an hour a day.
    (Man B)   What caused the blisters?
31. (Man A)   My headaches are terrible. Maybe I need more sleep.
    (Woman)   Actually, you need less sun and some aspirin. Plus it would help if you wore a hat. The sun is too bright.
    (Man B)   What caused the headache?

32. (Woman)   Annie invited me to Bill's house for Joe's birthday.
    (Man A)   You haven't forgotten my dinner party, have you?
    (Man B)   Whose house is the birthday party at?
33. (Man A)   You're a good height. Just a little plump.
    (Woman)   I wish I were taller. My hair would look longer if I were taller.
    (Man B)   What describes this woman?
34. (Man A)   I always begin my lectures with a joke. That puts the audience at ease.
    (Woman)   Then they laugh to put *you* at ease.
    (Man B)   How does the man like to begin?
35. (Woman)   This is the silliest book I have ever read. It's plain ridiculous.
    (Man A)   I've read duller books, though, but not one so long.
    (Man B)   How does the man feel about the book?

PART C

(Man A)   Questions 36 through 40 refer to the following lecture.
(Woman)   Bats, contrary to popular opinion, are not evil creatures. In fact, bats are extremely valuable because they eat an enormous amount of insects. In addition, they help to pollinate certain plants and spread the seeds of others. Bats, which are the only flying mammals, are divided into two groups according to their eating habits: those that eat insects and those that eat fruits and blossoms. Because bats generally live in caves and come out only at night, their habits were not studied for a long time and they were viewed with suspicion and fear.
    Many people are concerned that bats will settle in their hair, but actually a healthy bat will always avoid a collision. A

bat emits a high-pitched sound, which echoes from any object the sound hits. By this echo, the bat can tell what the object is and where it is. Unless your hair is full of insects, you never have to worry about a bat landing on your head. Unfortunately, these myths and fears have caused entire bat populations to be exterminated.

Fear is the bat's worst enemy. Farmers have been known to set fires in the caves where bats live and have killed tens of thousands of bats at one time. Today there is an increased interest in bats and an organization has been formed to help conserve the existing bat population of the world. Mass killings are not the only cause of the death of certain bat populations. The people of some cultures love to eat them. There is a big market for bat meat, which is considered a delicacy. Many countries have stopped the import and export of bats.

36. (Man B) How does the speaker describe the bat?

37. (Man B) What is used to classify bats?

38. (Man B) How does a bat locate an object?

39. (Man B) What is the bat's worst enemy?

40. (Man B) Why must bat populations be conserved?

(Man A) Questions 41 through 45 refer to the following dialog.

(Woman) Ships are still a widely used form of transportation.

(Man B) Yes, you tend to forget about them unless you live near water. But passengers and goods are still transported up and down rivers and across lakes, seas, and oceans. The advantage of water routes is that, unlike roads, they were already there; they didn't have to be made or maintained.

(Woman) When you look at water transportation historically, you can see why nations with strong navies were the most powerful. The Phoenicians and Greeks were famous for their shipping expertise. Their routes extended all the way from the Mediterranean to India and along the coasts of Africa.

(Man B) Good harbors had to be found or built, however, and there had to be wood available for ship building.

(Woman) That's why the United States dominated the market in the nineteenth century. The large forests provided ready resources for building swift sailing vessels, and cities like New York, Boston, and Baltimore have great harbors.

(Man B) Today, however, the high cost of American labor and ship construction has made it difficult for the United States to compete. Other countries now control the shipping lanes.

41. (Man A) According to the passage, what is a widely used form of transportation?

42. (Man A) What is the disadvantage of roads?

43. (Man A) In ancient times, which countries were the strongest?

44. (Man A) Why did the United States dominate the shipping market in the nineteenth century?

45. (Man B) Why is the United States no longer competitive in commercial shipping?

(Man A) Questions 46 through 50 refer to the following lecture.

(Woman) Some fifty years ago the world of art was elated with the shock of discovery. It was suddenly recognized that within the so-called dark continent a great art tradition had been flourishing for centuries. And it was observed that this African art anticipated in practice many of the most modern theories of artistic creation and technique.

For quite a while occasional African masks, wooden statues, ivories, and bronzes had been filtering back to Europe—the great British expedition to Benin in 1897 alone netted over two thousand bronzes, ivory, and wood carvings. But most of this art had been entombed in museum collections and forgotten by all but ethnologists. Europe and America had to grow in aesthetic theory before they could appreciate and understand African art, even though the technical excellence of African bronze casting was immediately recognized.

Today, however, thanks to the Cubist revolution, resulting in an entirely new aesthetic approach to works of art and our modern trend to cultural syncretism, it is no longer necessary to apologize for African art. It is universally recognized as one of the great artistic heritages of the world.

46. (Man B) What happened about 50 years ago?

47. (Man B) What important influence changed critics' attitudes toward African art?

48. (Man B) How long has Africa participated in artistic creation?

49. (Man B) How is African art considered in the modern world?

50. (Man B) What was historically recognized as an example of technical excellence?

PRACTICE TEST 4

PART A

1. (Man A) I beat the rug to get it clean, but the dust flew in my hair.

2. (Man B) Two boys started the marathon, and both finished.

3. (Woman) I had made reservations for 15, but there were 17 people in our party.

4. (Man A) Martin Luther King, Jr. had no intention of becoming so famous.

5. (Man B) Never in his life had the geologist seen anything like the Grand Canyon.

6. (Woman) The sports equipment that belongs to the school must be returned to the trainer at the end of the session.

7. (Man A) Because the sky was cloudy, no one was able to observe the eclipse.

8. (Man B) If the firemen had been called, they could have put out the fire.

9. (Woman) After I ate, I went to the movie, but Jim had already seen it, so he went to the store instead.

10. (Man A) The insurance coverage of Plan A is not as complete as that of Plan B but is more complete than Plan C.

11. (Man B) The widest part of the river is a few miles from here.

12. (Woman) The bus pulled away from the curb before the attendant loaded the bags.

13. (Man A) Since the absentee votes were not counted, the election is invalid.

14. (Man B) The batteries have been in the camera too long, and now the flash won't work.

15. (Woman) Having worked with that technician before, we were reluctant to give him more responsibility.

16. (Man A)   This error would never have occurred if the rules hadn't been ignored.
17. (Man B)   The problem wouldn't have become so serious if it had been dealt with sooner.
18. (Woman)   The committee established 30 recommendations for the Review Board to consider.
19. (Man A)   Even if we leave within the next half-hour, we'll still be too late for the ceremony.
20. (Man B)   The grain of the wood was gray, but I polished it anyway till it shone.

PART B

21. (Man A)   Can't you walk a little faster?
    (Woman)   This is the fastest I can.
    (Man B)   What does the man think about the woman?
22. (Woman)   Where have you been?
    (Man A)   I went for a walk, then decided to call on some friends.
    (Man B)   What did the man do first?
23. (Woman)   If you had listened to me, we'd be at the party by now. Move over. I'll drive.
    (Man A)   I was sure I knew how to get there. I'll turn around.
    (Man B)   What's the problem?
24. (Man A)   I gave the man full payment when he asked for it.
    (Woman)   No wonder he hasn't finished the job yet.
    (Man B)   Whom are they talking about?
25. (Woman)   Your nose is like your mother's.
    (Man A)   Yours is like your father's. My eyes are like my grandfather's!
    (Man B)   Whose nose does the woman's nose resemble?
26. (Man A)   Hand me the papers from my briefcase.
    (Woman)   Is that your briefcase there, next to the typewriter?
    (Man B)   What does he want?
27. (Man A)   How many classes are you taking?
    (Woman)   I've decided to take only one course and try to find a job.
    (Man B)   What will the woman do?

28. (Woman)   If your dog is eight, that's about 80 in human terms, right?
    (Man A)   No, it's seven human years to each year of a dog's life.
    (Man B)   How old is the dog?
29. (Man A)   I gave you two dollars. You've given me back 50 cents.
    (Woman)   That's right. The milk cost $1.50.
    (Man B)   How much change was there?
30. (Man A)   Those shoes you're wearing are a beautiful color.
    (Woman)   I know. It's your favorite. You always choose it, for ties, shirts, suits . . . everything.
    (Man B)   What does the man like?
31. (Woman)   You never should have gone out in the rain.
    (Man A)   I wouldn't have, but they were expecting me.
    (Man B)   What did the woman want the man to do?
32. (Man A)   You look much slimmer.
    (Woman)   I stopped eating bread last week.
    (Man B)   What happened to the woman?
33. (Woman)   If you had more experience, I'd hire you this minute.
    (Man A)   My supervisors will tell you that I learn very quickly!
    (Man B)   Where does this conversation take place?
34. (Man A)   Should we take out or eat in tonight?
    (Woman)   I'm too tired to cook.
    (Man B)   What does the woman mean?
35. (Woman)   If these prices get any higher, I'll have to go on a diet.
    (Man A)   You should anyway.
    (Man B)   What does the man mean?

PART C

(Man A)   Questions 36 through 40 refer to the following lecture.
(Man B)   Among the most exciting educational research findings of recent years is that human beings have "multiple intelligences." Prior to this study, people were considered either intelligent or not, based on the results of an IQ test.

However, we now know that a person's IQ reflects only a part of a person's "multiple intelligence." These are secrets just now being uncovered, and they help to explain how "smart" people can be "stupid," and vice versa. The reality is that we are smart in different ways and are smarter in some situations than in others.

36. (Woman) What general opinion preceded this study?

37. (Woman) What do the recent findings show?

38. (Woman) What does "multiple intelligences" refer to?

39. (Woman) What part does an IQ have in these findings?

40. (Woman) How does one explain "smart" people doing something "stupid"?

(Man A) Questions 41 through 45 refer to the following lecture.

(Man B) Carbohydrates are often considered to be less than nutritious, undesirable, or fattening. In fact, carbohydrates are essential in the diet to provide energy. This in turn permits proteins to be used for growth and maintenance of body cells. Carbohydrates are essential and should never be drastically cut from the diet.

Carbohydrates are named for their chemical composition: carbon, hydrogen, and oxygen. Through a highly complex mechanism involving the sun, air, and soil, plants store energy in the form of carbohydrates. Carbohydrates make up the supporting tissue of plants and are an important food for all animals, including humans.

When people eat cereal grains, fruits, and vegetables—rich sources of carbohydrates—they obtain energy directly at the rate of 4 calories per gram; when animals eat plants, humans benefit indirectly by eating meat. Carbohydrates from cereal grains represent the primary source of energy for many nations of the world.

41. (Woman) How are carbohydrates presented?

42. (Woman) What do carbohydrates provide?

43. (Woman) Which of the following is a rich source of carbohydrates?

44. (Woman) What is the primary source of energy internationally?

45. (Woman) What stores energy in the form of carbohydrates?

(Man A) Questions 46 through 50 refer to the following dialog.

(Woman) When most Americans think of the Gold Rush, they think of the discovery of gold in California in 1848. Prospectors, merchants, and adventurers from east of the Mississippi rushed west to California to make their fortunes.

(Man B) Very few of them became rich, though. It was hard work. City people from New York and Pennsylvania weren't used to working with their hands. It required a great deal of capital even to look for a mine, and if you were lucky enough to find one, then it took a great deal of money to take the gold out of the mine.

(Woman) The people who really made money were the men who provided the services for the gold seekers. Prospectors always needed tools, food, donkeys, horses, and mules.

(Man B)	Yes, the mule herder was probably the most wealthy man in the town. Everyone needed a mule.	46. (Man A)	Where was the 1848 Gold Rush?
(Woman)	It seems they could get by without a wife or a family, but they had to have a mule.	47. (Man A)	What was required to work a mine?
(Man B)	A few of the towns where gold was discovered are still inhabited. Most are ghost towns. No one lives there but wild animals.	48. (Man A)	According to the speakers, who profited the most from the Gold Rush?
		49. (Man A)	What did every prospector need?
		50. (Man A)	What has happened to most of the Gold Rush towns?

EXPLANATORY ANSWERS

PRACTICE TEST 1

SECTION 1

LISTENING COMPREHENSION

Part A

1. (A) Synonym: (A) is the closest in meaning. (B) similar sounds: *rather* and *father*; (C) similar sounds: *will fly* and *and I*; (D) is a contradiction of the statement.

2. (B) Comparison: (B) means the same, but uses a different vocabulary. (A) is a contradiction; (C) and (D) are true, but ignore the comparison with *walking*.

3. (C) Conditional: (C) is the closest in meaning to the statement. (A) similar sounds: *understand* and *stand*; (B) translates the first part of the statement too literally; (D) cannot be inferred from the information given.

4. (C) Chronological order: (C) means the same, but uses a different vocabulary. (A), (B), and (D) cannot be inferred from the information given.

5. (B) Contextual reference: (B) is a simplified version of the statement. (A) misinterprets the meaning of *follow* in this context; (C) and (D) cannot be inferred from the information given.

6. (B) Number discrimination: (B) is an inference of the statement. (A) similar sounds: *two movies* and *two of us*; (C) similar sounds: *afternoon* and *noon*; (D) similar sounds: *two movies* and *Tuesday*.

7. (C) Chronological order: (C) means the same, but uses a different vocabulary. (A) is a contradiction of the statement; (B) similar sounds: *last one off the bus* and *last bus*; (D) contradicts the statement.

8. (A) Synonym: (A) means the same, but uses a different vocabulary. (B), (C), and (D) cannot be inferred from the information given.

9. (A) Negation and Synonym: (A) means the same, but uses a different vocabulary. (B) confuses the meaning of the statement; (C) and (D) ask different questions.

10. (C) Chronological order: (C) means the same, but uses a different vocabulary. (A) confuses who moved; (B) offers a reason not contained in the statement; (D)

cannot be inferred from the information given.

11. (A) Contextual reference: (A) means the same, but uses a different vocabulary. (B) and (D) confuse the meaning of the statement; (C) is a contradiction of the statement.

12. (A) Conditional: (A) means the same, but uses a different vocabulary. (B) misinterprets the conditional for an action in the past; (C) confuses *I need* with *I'll buy*; (D) confuses the adverb *past* and the verb *past*.

13. (B) Contextual reference: (B) means the same, but uses a different vocabulary. (A) contradicts the statement; (C) cannot be inferred from the information given; (D) changes the meaning of the statement.

14. (D) Contextual reference: (D) means the same, but uses a different vocabulary. (A) and (C) focus on *up in the Athletic Office*; (B) confuses the homonyms *gym* and *Jim*.

15. (B) Comparison: (B) means the same, but uses a different vocabulary. (A), (C), and (D) cannot be inferred from the information given.

16. (B) Chronological order: (B) is a simplified version of the statement. (A) cannot be inferred from the information given; (C) confuses the meaning of *this afternoon* in this context; (D) confuses the meaning of *next Monday* in this context.

17. (A) Number discrimination: (A) means the same, but uses a different vocabulary. (B) is true, but it ignores important elements of the statement; (C) and (D) cannot be inferred from the information given.

18. (B) Comparison: (B) is a simplified version of the statement. (A) is a contradiction of the information given; (C) cannot be inferred from the information given; (D) confuses the meaning of *another* for *other*.

19. (D) Synonym: (D) means the same, but uses a different vocabulary. (A), (B), and (C) cannot be inferred from the information given.

20. (C) Synonym: (C) means the same, but uses a different vocabulary. (A) cannot be inferred from the information given; (B) is a contradiction of the statement; (D) similar sounds: *bookcase* for *book*.

Part B

21. (D) Contextual reference: (D) is an inference from the information given. The key words are *loan* and *officers*.
22. (B) Contextual reference: (B) the key words are *you've had that cold*. (D) confuses the noun *cold* (ailment) with the adjective *cold* (temperature).
23. (B) Contextual reference: (B) this dialogue forces the listener to focus on the main subject—*buses*.
24. (B) Chronological order: (B) the key clause is *I'll make some tea*. (A) and (C) cannot be inferred from the information given; (D) confuses the topic.
25. (C) Number discrimination: (C) the key words are *for Friday, too*. (B) ignores what the man says.
26. (A) Cause and effect: (A) is a simplified version of the statement. (B) confuses *try again* with *try harder*; (C) confuses *get a busy signal* with *get busy*; (D) is not mentioned.
27. (C) Chronological order: (C) the key words are *eat at 4* (compared with 5 or 6). (A) is a contradiction; (B) and (D) are not mentioned.
28. (B) Cause and effect: (B) is the logical conclusion. (A), (C), and (D) cannot be inferred from the information given.
29. (B) Synonym: (B) is the logical conclusion. (A) misinterprets *afraid we'll miss* for *afraid of*; (C) and (D) cannot be inferred from the information given.
30. (B) Synonym: (B) is a logical inference based on the information given. (A) and (C) cannot be inferred from the information given; (D) similar sounds: *card* with *car*; *forgot your glasses* with *forgot your car*.

31. (B) Contextual reference: (B) is a logical inference based on the key words. (A) and (C) cannot be inferred from the information given; (D) similar sounds: *officer* with *office*.
32. (A) Chronological order: (A) is another way of saying *retire*. (B) similar sounds: *retires* with *tires*; (C) cannot be inferred from the information given; (D) similar sounds: *walk out the door* with *take a walk*.
33. (C) Contextual reference: (C) is a logical inference based on the key words: *fill it up*, *oil*, and *pump*. (A), (B), and (D) cannot be inferred from the information given.
34. (A) Synonym: (A) is a logical inference based on the information given. (B) confuses who's traveling; (C) cannot be inferred from the information given; (D) confuses whose friend is arriving.
35. (C) Contextual reference: (C) is the only logical conclusion; key words are *reservations*, *room*. (A), (B), and (D) cannot be inferred from the information given.

Part C

36. (A) Mini-Talk
37. (D) Mini-Talk
38. (C) Mini-Talk
39. (C) Mini-Talk
40. (A) Mini-Talk
41. (B) Mini-Talk
42. (C) Dialog
43. (B) Dialog
44. (A) Dialog
45. (B) Dialog
46. (A) Mini-Talk
47. (D) Mini-Talk
48. (B) Mini-Talk
49. (C) Mini-Talk
50. (A) Mini-Talk

SECTION 2

STRUCTURE AND WRITTEN EXPRESSION

1. (B) Word families: *Traditionally*
2. (B) Prepositions: *different from*
3. (B) Adjective clauses: *in which participants have*; introduces adjective clause
4. (D) Verb: subject-verb agreement: *there is*; see *a potential*
5. (C) Articles: *the atmosphere*
6. (B) Verb: inappropriate tense: *experiencing*; see *are . . ..*
7. (B) Parallel structures: *not just (not only) . . . but*
8. (D) Active/passive verbs: *composed*; see *were*
9. (A) Pronouns: agreement: *its*
10. (A) Verb: inappropriate tense: *they produced*; see *were losing*
11. (B) Noun clauses: *that* (object of believe)
12. (A) Pronouns: agreement: *their*; agrees with *residents and visitors*

142 Explanatory Answers

13. (C) Parallel structures: *economically*; see *environmentally and*
14. (D) Active/passive verbs: *was established*
15. (D) Adverb clauses: *While*
16. (B) Verb: subject-verb agreement: *writer is*
17. (C) Verb omitted: *they have little sense*
18. (C) Adjective clauses: omit; *are still*
19. (A) Word families: *unlike*
20. (A) Verb: inappropriate tense: *drink*
21. (C) Verb: subject-verb agreement: *groups . . . check*
22. (B) Gerunds: *by* (preposition) *checking*
23. (B) Verb: inappropriate tense: *known*
24. (D) Pronouns: agreement: *songbirds . . ..their own*
25. (B) Word order: adjective/adverb placement: *growing need*
26. (B) Comparisons: *too thin*
27. (C) Word families: *health care*
28. (B) Adjective clauses: *and are capable*
29. (B) Verb: subject-verb agreement: *Leaves have*
30. (C) Word families: *may live*
31. (C) Verb: inappropriate tense: *exposure* or *exposing animals*
32. (A) Subject repeated: omit *they*
33. (C) Pronouns: agreement: *its way*
34. (A) Adjective clauses: *Consumers spend*
35. (B) Word order: adjective/adverb placement: *electric elevator*
36. (C) Verb omitted: *that does not spoil*
37. (C) Infinitives: *to reduce*
38. (D) Articles: *the ocean*
39. (A) Word families: *Contrary*
40. (A) Comparatives: *the longest*

SECTION 3

READING COMPREHENSION AND VOCABULARY

1. (C)
2. (B)
3. (D)
4. (A)
5. (B)
6. (B)
7. (D)
8. (B)
9. (C)
10. (B)
11. (D)
12. (A)
13. (B)
14. (C)
15. (A)
16. (C)
17. (B)
18. (A)
19. (B)
20. (D)
21. (D)
22. (C)
23. (C)
24. (A)
25. (B)
26. (B)
27. (D)
28. (B)
29. (C)
30. (A)

31. (A) Factual: positive
32. (B) Factual: positive
33. (A) Factual: positive
34. (B) Inference: specific
35. (B) Factual: positive
36. (A) Factual: positive
37. (A) Factual: positive
38. (B) Factual: negative
39. (C) Factual: positive
40. (A) Factual: positive
41. (A) Factual: positive
42. (C) Inference: specific
43. (C) Factual: positive
44. (A) Factual: positive
45. (D) Main idea
46. (C) Inference: general
47. (A) Viewpoint
48. (B) Inference: specific
49. (C) Factual: positive
50. (D) Factual: positive
51. (A) Factual: positive
52. (B) Main idea
53. (B) Main idea
54. (B) Inference: general
55. (B) Factual: positive
56. (C) Factual: positive
57. (B) Factual: positive
58. (D) Factual: positive
59. (A) Factual: positive
60. (A) Inference: general

PRACTICE TEST 2

SECTION 1

LISTENING COMPREHENSION

Part A

1. **(B)** Synonym: (B) is the closest in meaning. (A) asks *where*; (C) asks *how long*; (D) asks for a reason for the delay.

2. **(D)** Negation: (D) offers a reason why the man hasn't received his two newspapers. (A) cannot be inferred from the information given; (B) similar sounds; *receive* and *receipt*; (C) confuses *newspapers* with *days*.

3. **(D)** Number discrimination: (D) means the same, but uses a different vocabulary. (A) cannot be inferred from the information given; (B) confuses the preposition *on* as indicating location; (C) ignores *exam* and confuses the meaning of *first*.

4. **(A)** Conditional: (A) means the same, but uses a different vocabulary. (B) focuses on the negative *don't*; (C) confuses the condition, *If you are hungry*; (D) focuses on *why don't you* and contradicts the meaning of the original statement.

5. **(D)** Number discrimination: (D) is a simplified version of the statement. (A) similar sounds: *ten dollars* and *ten people*; (B) similar sounds: *ten dollars* and *ten miles*; (C) misinterprets the direction of the ride.

6. **(C)** Synonym: (C) means the same, but uses a different vocabulary. (A) and (B) focus on *how*, but misinterpret its meaning; (D) similar sounds: *afternoon* and *noon*.

7. **(B)** Cause and effect: (C) is a simplified version of the statement. (A) similar sounds: *housework* and *homework*; (C) cannot be inferred from the information given; (D) mixes up the tenses; confuses the meaning of the statement.

8. **(A)** Synonym: (A) is a simplified version of the statement. (B) similar sounds: *train* and *plane*; confuses the time element; (C) similar sounds: *train* and *rain*; (D) confuses the meaning of the statement; similar sounds: *train* and *grain*.

9. **(C)** Chronological order: (C) means the same, but uses a different vocabulary. (A) confuses the meaning of the statement; (B) similar sounds: *woke* and *walk*; (D) is a contradiction of the statement.

10. **(D)** Synonym: (D) means the same, but uses a different vocabulary. (A) similar sounds: *park* and *parking*; *reserved* and *preserved*; (B) confuses the meaning of the

statement; (C) focuses on *reserved* and misinterprets its meaning.

11. **(C)** Synonym: (C) means the same, but uses a different vocabulary. (A) confuses the meaning of the statement; (B) confuses the tenses of the verbs; (D) focuses on the books as opposed to the action of Richard's returning them.

12. **(D)** Chronological order: (D) is a simplified version of the directions given. (A) is not a direction; (B) and (C) confuse the meaning of the statement.

13. **(A)** Number discrimination: (A) is the closest in meaning. (B) similar sounds: *counted* and *count on*; (C) and (D) confuse the meaning of the statement.

14. **(B)** Number discrimination: (B) is the only truthful option. (A), (C), and (D) confuse the numbers.

15. **(B)** Synonym: (B) means the same, but uses a different vocabulary. (A) misinterprets *out of order*; (C) and (D) similar sounds: *phone* and *loan*.

16. **(B)** Synonym: (B) means the same, but uses a different vocabulary. (A) confuses the noun and participle form of *building*; (C) and (D) cannot be inferred from the information given.

17. **(D)** Chronological order: (D) is the only truthful option. (A), (B), and (C) confuse the meaning of the statement.

18. **(B)** Chronological order: (B) means the same, but uses a different vocabulary. (A) cannot be inferred from the information given; (C) similar sounds: *moving* and *movie*; (D) confuses the meaning of the statement.

19. **(B)** Negation: (B) is the closest in meaning. (A) is an inference, but too impersonal; (C) and (D) cannot be inferred from the information given.

20. **(D)** Conditional: (D) is a simplified version of the statement. (A) and (B) are contradictions of the statement. (C) similar sounds: *glass* and *the grass*.

Part B

21. **(C)** Contextual reference: (C) is an inference from the information given. (A) and (D) cannot be inferred from the information given; (B) is a contradiction.

22. **(A)** Contextual reference: (A) The key words are *calculator* and *calculation skills*. (B),

(C), and (D) are not related to these key words.

23. (B) Contextual reference: (B) This dialog forces the listener to focus on the main subject, the glasses. (A) is not mentioned; (C) is heard as part of *bookcase*; (D) is mentioned as a possible place to find the glasses.

24. (D) Cause and effect: (D) The key clause is *but I don't have time*. (A) and (B) cannot be inferred from the information given; (C) misinterprets *but I don't have time* as referring to chronological time.

25. (B) Contextual reference: (B) The key words are *mail a package and buy some stamps*. (A) and (D) may have picked up *buy*, but not *stamps*; (C) misinterprets *lamps* for *stamps*.

26. (A) Negation: (A) The key phrase is *Another rejection letter!* (B) and (C) cannot be inferred from the information given; (D) confuses the meaning of the statement.

27. (C) Contextual reference: (C) The key words are *check cashing, deposits, withdrawals*. (A) and (B) are possible places where *lines* occur, but do not include the key words; (D) is unrelated to the information given.

28. (D) Contextual reference: (D) is a logical conclusion. (A), (B), and (C) cannot be inferred from the information given.

29. (C) Contextual reference: (C) A stationery store sells paper products. (A) misinterprets *use some air* for putting air in tires (possibly); (C) picks up on *use some air* as referring to an air conditioner; (D) may interpret *I'll run* as a sport, as in jogging.

30. (A) Synonym: (A) The key words are *Congratulations* and *grade*. (B) is a contradiction; (C) picks up on earned, but interprets it with money; (D) cannot be inferred from the information given.

31. (D) Cause and effect: (D) is a logical inference based on the information given. (A) is a contradiction; (B) cannot be inferred from the information given; (C) picks up on the word *due*, but misinterprets the meaning in the original statement.

32. (A) Contextual reference: (A) is the only logical conclusion. (B) cannot be inferred from the information given; the subjects of (C) and (D) are mentioned, but the meanings cannot be inferred from the information given.

33. (D) Contextual reference: (D) The key words are *one-way or round-trip ticket*. (A), (B), and (C) cannot be inferred from the information given.

34. (C) Contextual reference: (C) The key word is *month*, which equals approximately 4 weeks. (A), (B), and (D) are miscalculations.

35. (C) Contextual reference: (C) is the only logical conclusion. (A) and (D) cannot be inferred from the information given; (B) equates *money* with *change*, which isn't true.

Part C

36. (A) Dialog
37. (C) Dialog
38. (B) Dialog
39. (A) Dialog
40. (A) Dialog
41. (B) Mini-Talk
42. (B) Mini-Talk
43. (D) Mini-Talk
44. (A) Mini-Talk
45. (A) Mini-Talk
46. (C) Dialog
47. (B) Dialog
48. (A) Dialog
49. (A) Dialog
50. (B) Dialog

SECTION 2

STRUCTURE AND WRITTEN EXPRESSION

1. (C) Prepositions: *required of*
2. (B) Verb: inappropriate tense: *happened*; see *ago*
3. (D) Prepositions: *between*
4. (A) Comparisons: *a greater number of*; see *than*
5. (D) Pronouns: form: *one*; see *only*
6. (B) Word order: adjective/adverb placement: *no single food*
7. (C) Infinitives: *to exchange*; see *agreed*
8. (B) Infinitives: *to be*; see *acknowledged*
9. (D) Comparisons: *the smallest*
10. (D) Parallel structures: *begin*; see *will arrive at . . and*
11. (D) Word families: adjective: *historical*
12. (C) Participle form: *known*
13. (B) Gerunds: *Manufacturing*
14. (B) Parallel structures: *has produced*; see *has consumed*
15. (C) Verb: inappropriate tense: *are caused*
16. (A) Word families: adjective: *high*

17. (B) Verb: unnecessary form: *needs to*
18. (D) Word order: adjective/adverb placement: *citizenship* here is adjective: *citizenship training*
19. (C) Comparisons: *the longest*
20. (A) Word families: *annually*
21. (B) Parallel structures: *percent* is singular: *80 percent fat*
22. (C) Word families: *usually*
23. (A) Word order: adjective/adverb placement: *natural beauty*
24. (C) Verb omitted: *are restricted* or *should be restricted*
25. (C) Gerunds: see *practice of printing . . . and selling*
26. (D) Word families: *second*
27. (A) Subject repeated: *films were first made*
28. (B) Pronouns: agreement: *geologists . . . their predictions*
29. (C) Verb: subject-verb agreement: *The establishment . . . provides*
30. (B) Verb: subject-verb agreement: *The . . . melting . . . is*
31. (A) Word families: noun: *invention*
32. (B) Subject repeated: omit *it*
33. (B) Infinitives: *easy to handle*
34. (D) Pronouns: agreement: *Babies . . . their*
35. (D) Verb tense: inappropriate tense: *did*; see *ago*
36. (C) Word families: adjective: *available*
37. (D) Verb: subject-verb agreement: *the . . . points . . . are*
38. (D) Participle form: past participle in adj. phrase: *known*
39. (C) Participle form: adjective: *established*
40. (B) Verb: subject-verb agreement: *people find*

SECTION 3

READING COMPREHENSION AND VOCABULARY

1. (C)
2. (A)
3. (D)
4. (A)
5. (C)
6. (D)
7. (A)
8. (A)
9. (D)
10. (D)
11. (D)
12. (B)
13. (B)
14. (A)
15. (B)
16. (C)
17. (C)
18. (A)
19. (D)
20. (A)
21. (A)
22. (C)
23. (C)
24. (A)
25. (D)
26. (C)
27. (C)
28. (A)
29. (C)
30. (A)

31. (C) Main idea
32. (A) Inference: general
33. (D) Factual: positive
34. (A) Factual: positive
35. (C) Factual: positive
36. (C) Factual: positive
37. (B) Inference: specific
38. (C) Factual: positive
39. (C) Written expression
40. (B) Main idea
41. (B) Factual: positive
42. (B) Inference: general
43. (C) Organization
44. (D) Inference: general
45. (A) Factual: positive
46. (C) Factual: positive
47. (D) Main idea
48. (B) Factual: positive
49. (B) Factual: positive
50. (A) Written expression
51. (A) Factual: positive
52. (D) Factual: positive
53. (B) Factual: positive
54. (C) Factual: negative
55. (B) Factual: positive
56. (D) Written expression
57. (A) Factual: positive
58. (A) Main idea
59. (B) Viewpoint
60. (D) Follow-on

PRACTICE TEST 3

SECTION 1

LISTENING COMPREHENSION

Part A

1. (C) Contextual reference: (C) is a simplified version of the statement. (A) similar sounds: *plane* and *train*; (B) misinterprets *flew*; (D) is true, but unrelated to the statement.
2. (C) Number discrimination: (C) is a summary of the statement. (A) is a contradiction; (B) and (D) are false implications.
3. (B) Similar sounds: (B) is a simplified version of the statement. (A) similar sounds: *dress* and *distress*; (C) similar sounds: *dress* and *address*; (D) similar sounds: *tore* and *store*; *down* and *town*.
4. (A) Negation: (A) is a summary of the sentence. (B), (C), and (D) are contradictions of the statement.
5. (A) Negation: (A) is a simplified version of the statement. (B) cannot be inferred from the information given; (C) is unrelated; (D) is a contradiction of the statement.
6. (C) Chronological order: (C) is the only truthful option. (A) and (B) are contradictions to the statement; (D) confuses the meaning of the statement.
7. (D) Cause and effect: (D) is an inference; key words are *protect, downpour*. (A) and (B) incorrectly focus on *blanket*; (C) is a contradiction of the statement.
8. (B) Synonym: (B) means the same, but uses a different vocabulary. (A) similar sounds: *reason* and *raisins*; (C) similar sounds: *display* and *play*; (D) confuses the meaning of the statement.
9. (C) Synonym: (C) means the same, but uses a different vocabulary. (A) and (D) are unrelated to the statement; (B) similar sounds: *weep* and *sweep*.
10. (D) Contextual reference: (D) is the closest in meaning to the statement. (A) and (B) focus only on *five* and not its referent; (C) cannot be inferred from the information given.
11. (D) Contextual reference: (D) is an inference; key words are *only one of the bills*. (A) incorrectly focuses on *grain*; (B) similar sounds: *bills* and *Bill*; (C) is not related to the information in the statement; similar sounds: *grain* and *rain*.
12. (A) Synonym: (A) means the same, but uses a different vocabulary. (B) and (C) cannot

be inferred from the information given; (D) is unrelated to the statement.
13. (A) Number discrimination: (A) is a summary of the statement. (B) is a miscalculation; (C) and (D) are contradictions.
14. (C) Conditional: (C) is a simplified version of the statement. (A) incorrectly focuses on *triple*; (B) cannot be inferred from the information given; (D) is unrelated to the statement.
15. (C) Conditional: (C) is a summary of the statement. (A) is a misinterpretation of *support* and possibly *motion*; (B) is unrelated to the statement, and (D) confuses the meaning of *motion*.
16. (B) Contextual reference: (B) is a summary of the statement. (A) and (C) cannot be inferred from the information given; (D) similar sounds: *enlisted* and *list*.
17. (C) Conditional: (C) is a simplified version of the statement. (A) and (B) are unrelated to the statement; (D) cannot be inferred from the information given.
18. (D) Synonym: (D) is a simplified version of the statement. (A) and (B) focus on *error* as a synonym for *mistake*, but are unrelated to the meaning of the statement; (C) is also unrelated.
19. (D) Contextual reference: (D) is the only truthful option. (A) and (C) are contradictions of the statement; (B) cannot be inferred from the information given.
20. (A) Contextual reference: (A) is the only truthful option. (B) and (C) cannot be inferred from the information given; (D) is a contradiction of the statement.

Part B

21. (A) Synonym: (A) means the same as *That's too bad*. The other options are incorrect interpretations.
22. (B) Number discrimination: (B) This question forces the listener to focus on a detail—*how many hours*. (A), (C), and (D) are numbers referred to in other parts of the dialog.
23. (C) Number discrimination: (C) The listener must focus on one detail—*which bus*. (A), (B), and (D) are miscalculations or misinterpretations.

24. **(C)** Synonym: (C) This dialog focuses on the meaning of *exhausted*. (A), (B), and (D) do not explain the vocabulary focus.
25. **(D)** Contextual reference: (D) is the logical conclusion. (A) and (B) are contradictions; (C) is not mentioned in the dialog.
26. **(B)** Contextual reference: (B) From the phrase, *my father's family*. (A), (C), and (D) are incorrect.
27. **(A)** Similar sounds: (A) is the only truthful option. (B) similar sounds: *trash* and *rash*; (C) is unrelated; (D) cannot be inferred from the information given.
28. **(C)** Comparison: (C) is the logical conclusion. (A) presumes they both have an opinion of the other restaurant; (B) is a contradiction; (D) cannot be inferred from the information given.
29. **(A)** Chronological order: (A) This question asks the listener to focus on the sequence of events. (B) happened second; (C) will have happened last; (D) is the next to the last event.
30. **(C)** Cause and effect: (C) is a logical conclusion; key words are *are too new; I even wore*. (A) and (B) would not be the cause of blisters; (D) is not mentioned in the dialog.
31. **(D)** Cause and effect: (D) The clause, *you need less sun* indicates the cause of the headache. (A) indicates a misunderstanding of the dialog; (B) is his suggestion; (C) is offered as a solution.
32. **(C)** Contextual reference: (C) This question focuses on a detail—*whose house*. The other options are incorrect.
33. **(B)** Synonym: (B) is the only truthful option. (A) and (D) are contradictions; (C) is not mentioned.
34. **(A)** Contextual reference: (A) is a paraphrase of a joke. (B) is not mentioned in the dialog; (C) and (D) are misinterpretations.
35. **(C)** Contextual reference: (C) is the logical conclusion; key phrase is *but not one so long*. (A) is a contradiction; (B) is the woman's opinion; (D) incorrectly focuses on the woman's phrase, *plain ridiculous*.

Part C

36. **(B)** Mini-Talk
37. **(D)** Mini-Talk
38. **(C)** Mini-Talk
39. **(C)** Mini-Talk
40. **(B)** Mini-Talk
41. **(A)** Dialog
42. **(B)** Dialog
43. **(A)** Dialog
44. **(C)** Dialog
45. **(B)** Dialog
46. **(D)** Mini-Talk
47. **(B)** Mini-Talk
48. **(D)** Mini-Talk
49. **(B)** Mini-Talk
50. **(A)** Mini-Talk

SECTION 2

STRUCTURE AND WRITTEN EXPRESSION

1. **(C)** Adjective clauses: *who is* (*who* takes singular verb)
2. **(B)** Pronouns: agreement: *their* (*police* is considered plural)
3. **(A)** Prepositions: *on the frontier*
4. **(D)** Conditionals: *Unless there is a snowstorm*
5. **(D)** Parallel structures: joining two adjectives with correct conjunction: *fast and efficient*
6. **(C)** Verb: inappropriate tense; present perfect: (*calculators*) *have proved*
7. **(D)** Participle form: *rapidly expanding*
8. **(A)** Word order: subject-verb: *what the priority should be*
9. **(D)** Comparisons (equality): *as well as*
10. **(C)** Word families: adjective: *equal*
11. **(B)** Verb: inappropriate tense: simple present: *believe*
12. **(C)** Adjective clauses: marker + verb: *who is*
13. **(A)** Adverb clauses: *Even though many do not want*
14. **(B)** Adjective clauses: *whose origin remains obscure*
15. **(D)** Gerunds: *After hearing*
16. **(A)** Verb: unnecessary form: delete *being*
17. **(C)** Verb: subject-verb agreement: *believe*
18. **(A)** Verb omitted: *to be: who are always*
19. **(D)** Pronouns: agreement: *on her head*
20. **(D)** Parallel structures: *by inhibiting them*
21. **(A)** Verb omitted: *was preserved*
22. **(D)** Verb: inappropriate tense: see *is brought: explodes*
23. **(A)** Reduced adjective clauses: *substances produced*
24. **(B)** Word order: adjective/adverb placement: *potters are seldom*
25. **(C)** Adverb clauses: *because the food*
26. **(B)** Parallel structures: *and driving/being in traffic jams*
27. **(B)** Infinitives: *to imagine*
28. **(D)** Verb omitted: *the Nile was three times*
29. **(D)** Parallel structures: *as the least*
30. **(C)** Parallel structures: *than the lion*
31. **(B)** Pronouns: form: *enabling them to work*
32. **(D)** Prepositions: *of the school*

33. (C) Gerunds: *out of traveling*; or noun; *travel*
34. (A) Subject repeated: *Since first being performed*
35. (A) Adverb clauses: *Even though the African tsetse*
36. (B) Parallel structures: *the appearance but the sounds*
37. (A) Subject repeated: *which will be torn down*
38. (B) Word order: adjective/adverb placement: *that organized sports*
39. (C) Verb: inappropriate tense: *than is*; see *currently*
40. (B) Subject repeated: *should include*

SECTION 3
READING COMPREHENSION AND VOCABULARY

1.. (B)
2. (C)
3. (C)
4. (B)
5. (D)
6. (A)
7. (A)
8. (B)
9. (B)
10. (A)
11. (C)
12. (A)
13. (A)
14. (B)
15. (C)
16. (A)
17. (B)
18. (D)
19. (B)
20. (A)
21. (A)
22. (B)
23. (D)
24. (B)
25. (A)
26. (C)
27. (A)
28. (A)
29. (B)
30. (C)

31. (C) Factual: positive
32. (D) Factual: positive
33. (B) Factual: positive
34. (B) Main idea
35. (B) Organization
36. (A) Main idea
37. (D) Inference: specific
38. (B) Written expression
39. (C) Written expression
40. (A) Factual: positive
41. (C) Factual: positive
42. (C) Viewpoint
43. (C) Factual: positive
44. (B) Inference: general
45. (C) Organization
46. (C) Viewpoint
47. (A) Written expression
48. (B) Main idea
49. (A) Inference: specific
50. (D) Inference: specific
51. (B) Factual: positive
52. (A) Follow-on
53. (C) Written expression
54. (B) Main idea
55. (B) Factual: positive
56. (B) Factual: positive
57. (A) Inference: general
58. (B) Analogy
59. (B) Follow-on
60. (C) Viewpoint

PRACTICE TEST 4

SECTION 1

LISTENING COMPREHENSION

Part A

1. (C) Cause and effect: (C) is a simplified version of the statement. (A) is unrelated to the statement; (B) similar sounds: *rug* and *bug*; (D) is a contradiction of the statement.
2. (A) Number discrimination: (A) is a summary of the statement. (B) and (D) are not mentioned; (C) cannot be inferred from the information given.
3. (B) Number discrimination: (B) is a simplified version of the statement. (A), (C), and (D) confuse the numbers.
4. (A) Synonym: (A) means the same, but uses a different vocabulary. (B) and (C) are contradictions of the statement; (D) cannot be inferred from the information given.
5. (D) Negation: (D) is a summary of the statement. (A) and (C) are contradictions of the statement; (B) cannot be inferred from the information given.
6. (D) Contextual reference: (D) is a simplified version of the statement. (A), (B), and (C) cannot be inferred from the information given.
7. (C) Synonym: (C) means the same, but uses a different vocabulary. (A) and (B) incorrectly focus on *eclipse*; (D) is a contradiction of the statement.
8. (D) Conditional: (D) is the logical conclusion. (A) and (B) are contradictions of the statement; (C) is a confusion of the statement.
9. (A) Chronological order: (A) This question tests the listener's ability to follow a sequence of events. (B) and (C) are contradictions; (D) cannot be inferred from the information given.
10. (B) Contextual reference: (B) is the closest in meaning to the statement. (A), (C), and (D) are contradictions of the statement.
11. (D) Contextual reference: (D) means the same, but uses a different vocabulary. (A) is a contradiction; (B) and (C) similar sounds: *mile* and *smile*.
12. (C) Chronological order: (C) is a summary of the statement. (A) is a contradiction; (B) and (D) are unrelated to the statement.
13. (D) Conditional: (D) is a summary of the statement. All other options are unrelated to the statement.
14. (B) Cause and effect: (B) is a summary of the statement. (A), (C), and (D) incorrectly focus on *too long*.
15. (C) Synonym: (C) is a summary of the statement. (A) and (D) cannot be inferred from the information given; (B) is unrelated to the statement.
16. (B) Conditional: (B) is a summary of the statement. (A) and (C) are contradictions; (D) cannot be inferred from the information given.
17. (C) Conditional: (C) is a simplified version of the statement. (A) cannot be inferred from the information given; (B) is unrelated to the statement; (D) is a contradiction.
18. (B) Number discrimination: (B) is a simplified version of the statement. (A), (C), and (D) confuse the meaning of the statement.
19. (D) Synonym: (D) is the only truthful option. (A) and (C) are contradictions of the statement; (B) cannot be inferred from the information given.
20. (D) Contextual reference: (D) is a summary of the first part of the statement. (A) and (B) are unrelated to the meaning of the statement; (C) cannot be inferred from the information given.

Part B

21. (A) Contextual reference: (A) The question *Can't you walk a little faster?* implies the woman walks slowly. (B) and (D) are contradictions.
22. (C) Chronological order: (C) This question forces the listener to focus on a sequence. (A) happens last; (B) and (D) aren't mentioned.
23. (D) Synonym: (D) is the logical conclusion. (A), (B), and (C) are misinterpretations.
24. (B) Contextual reference: (B) is the logical conclusion; key words are *finished the job*. (A), (C), and (D) do not relate to the dialog.
25. (D) Contextual reference: (D) The listener must focus on a detail—*the woman's nose*. The other options are incorrect.
26. (D) Contextual reference: (D) From the clause, *Hand me my papers*. (A), (B), and (C) are incorrect.

27. (A) Chronological order: (A) is the only truthful option. (B) similar sounds: *course* for *cruise*; (C) and (D) are unrelated.

28. (B) Number discrimination: (B) From the clause, *If your dog is eight*. (A) refers to seven human years; (C) and (D) are unrelated to the statement.

29. (A) Number discrimination; (A) From . . . *given me back 50 cents*. (B) is unrelated; (C) was the cost of the milk; (D) is the amount of money given.

30. (B) Contextual reference: (B) Key words are *a beautiful color . . . It's your favorite*. The other options are incorrect.

31. (C) Negation: (C) From the clause, *you never should have gone out*. (A) and (B) are contradictions; (D) is confused and similar sounds: *rain* for *train*.

32. (D) Cause and effect: (D) is the logical conclusion; key words are *You look much slimmer*. The other options are not mentioned.

33. (C) Contextual reference: (C) is the best answer. (A), (B), and (D) are not feasible in this context.

34. (C) Synonym: (C) means the same, but uses a different vocabulary. (A) cannot be inferred from the information given; (B) and (D) are misinterpretations.

35. (D) Cause and effect: (D) is the logical conclusion; key phrase is *you should anyway*. (A) and (B) are unrelated; (C) is a contradiction.

Part C

36. (A) Mini-Talk
37. (D) Mini-Talk
38. (B) Mini-Talk
39. (A) Mini-Talk
40. (A) Mini-Talk
41. (B) Mini-Talk
42. (D) Mini-Talk
43. (B) Mini-Talk
44. (A) Mini-Talk
45. (B) Mini-Talk
46. (A) Dialog
47. (B) Dialog
48. (D) Dialog
49. (C) Dialog
50. (A) Dialog

SECTION 2
STRUCTURE AND WRITTEN EXPRESSION

1. (B) Verb: inappropriate tense: *dissolves*
2. (C) Word order: adjective/adverb placement: *The work of that artist*
3. (A) Comparisons: *faster*
4. (C) Pronouns: agreement: *rats . . . their*
5. (A) Conditionals: present unreal: *would be*
6. (C) Adverb clauses: marker: *because*
7. (D) Parallel structures: see *either . . . or*
8. (B) Gerunds: object of preposition: *After exploding*
9. (D) Word order: adjective/adverb placement: *are probably more common*
10. (B) Adjective clauses: *is the best time to harvest*
11. (C) Word families: noun: *generator*
12. (D) Noun clauses: marker: *what*
13. (A) Active/passive voice: *was caused by*
14. (B) Participle form: *(which is) accumulating*
15. (D) Subjective: *direct* (see *requests*)
16. (B) Subject repeated: delete *they*
17. (D) Word families: *temporary*
18. (A) Active/passive verbs: *After being given*
19. (B) Pronouns: agreement: *the Spanish . . . their*
20. (D) Verb: inappropriate tense: *who died . . . abandoned*

21. (C) Verb: inappropriate tense: *is expected* or *can be expected*
22. (D) Pronouns: agreement: *themselves*
23. (B) Noun clauses: conjunction: *that the tomb*
24. (B) Parallel structures: *both . . . and*
25. (B) Articles: *horsehair* or *a horsehair*
26. (B) Comparisons: *thinner*
27. (D) Conditionals: *would decrease*
28. (C) Parallel structures: *and security*
29. (B) Verb: unnecessary form: delete *did*
30. (A) Verb: inappropriate form: simple present: *makes*
31. (C) Word order: adjective/adverb placement: *is seldom acclaimed*
32. (B) Prepositions: *belief in individualism*
33. (B) Reduced adjective clauses: *coming*
34. (B) Adjective clauses: marker omissions: *additives which will reduce*
35. (D) Parallel structures: adjective: *aggressive*
36. (C) Verb: subject-verb agreement: *blood cells . . . are stored*
37. (C) Adjective clauses: marker omission: *which/who had been*
38. (D) Infinitives: *to return*
39. (A) Verb omitted: *who had been*
40. (D) Verb omitted: *as the death rate did* or *as did the death rate*

SECTION 3

READING COMPREHENSION AND VOCABULARY

1. (A)	31. (B)	Main idea
2. (B)	32. (C)	Factual: positive
3. (C)	33. (B)	Inference: specific
4. (A)	34. (C)	Written expression
5. (D)	35. (B)	Viewpoint
6. (A)	36. (A)	Organization
7. (A)	37. (A)	Written expression
8. (C)	38. (C)	Main idea
9. (B)	39. (B)	Viewpoint
10. (A)	40. (D)	Inference: general
11. (A)	41. (B)	Written expression
12. (C)	42. (B)	Organization
13. (B)	43. (C)	Follow-on
14. (A)	44. (D)	Main idea
15. (B)	45. (B)	Factual: positive
16. (D)	46. (A)	Factual: positive
17. (B)	47. (D)	Factual: negative
18. (B)	48. (C)	Main idea
19. (C)	49. (C)	Viewpoint
20. (C)	50. (D)	Organization
21. (D)	51. (B)	Main idea
22. (A)	52. (C)	Factual: positive
23. (C)	53. (D)	Factual: negative
24. (A)	54. (B)	Inference: general
25. (D)	55. (B)	Viewpoint
26. (C)	56. (D)	Follow-on
27. (B)	57. (C)	Main idea
28. (C)	58. (A)	Factual: positive
29. (D)	59. (C)	Inference: specific
30. (D)	60. (B)	Written expression

ANSWER SHEETS

Answer Sheet for Practice Test 1

Tear this sheet out and use it to mark your answers.

SECTION 1
LISTENING
COMPREHENSION

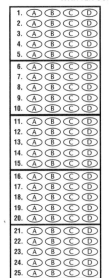

SECTION 2
STRUCTURE AND
WRITTEN COMPREHENSION

SECTION 1
READING COMPREHENSION
AND VOCABULARY

Answer Sheet for Practice Test 2

Tear this sheet out and use it to mark your answers.

SECTION 1
LISTENING
COMPREHENSION

SECTION 2
STRUCTURE AND
WRITTEN COMPREHENSION

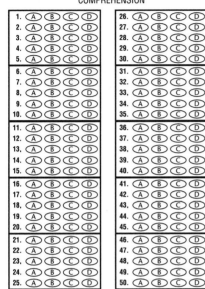

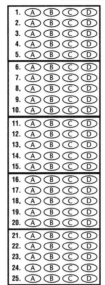

SECTION 1
READING COMPREHENSION
AND VOCABULARY

Answer Sheet for Practice Test 3

Tear this sheet out and use it to mark your answers.

SECTION 1
LISTENING COMPREHENSION

1. Ⓐ Ⓑ Ⓒ Ⓓ	26. Ⓐ Ⓑ Ⓒ Ⓓ
2. Ⓐ Ⓑ Ⓒ Ⓓ	27. Ⓐ Ⓑ Ⓒ Ⓓ
3. Ⓐ Ⓑ Ⓒ Ⓓ	28. Ⓐ Ⓑ Ⓒ Ⓓ
4. Ⓐ Ⓑ Ⓒ Ⓓ	29. Ⓐ Ⓑ Ⓒ Ⓓ
5. Ⓐ Ⓑ Ⓒ Ⓓ	30. Ⓐ Ⓑ Ⓒ Ⓓ
6. Ⓐ Ⓑ Ⓒ Ⓓ	31. Ⓐ Ⓑ Ⓒ Ⓓ
7. Ⓐ Ⓑ Ⓒ Ⓓ	32. Ⓐ Ⓑ Ⓒ Ⓓ
8. Ⓐ Ⓑ Ⓒ Ⓓ	33. Ⓐ Ⓑ Ⓒ Ⓓ
9. Ⓐ Ⓑ Ⓒ Ⓓ	34. Ⓐ Ⓑ Ⓒ Ⓓ
10. Ⓐ Ⓑ Ⓒ Ⓓ	35. Ⓐ Ⓑ Ⓒ Ⓓ
11. Ⓐ Ⓑ Ⓒ Ⓓ	36. Ⓐ Ⓑ Ⓒ Ⓓ
12. Ⓐ Ⓑ Ⓒ Ⓓ	37. Ⓐ Ⓑ Ⓒ Ⓓ
13. Ⓐ Ⓑ Ⓒ Ⓓ	38. Ⓐ Ⓑ Ⓒ Ⓓ
14. Ⓐ Ⓑ Ⓒ Ⓓ	39. Ⓐ Ⓑ Ⓒ Ⓓ
15. Ⓐ Ⓑ Ⓒ Ⓓ	40. Ⓐ Ⓑ Ⓒ Ⓓ
16. Ⓐ Ⓑ Ⓒ Ⓓ	41. Ⓐ Ⓑ Ⓒ Ⓓ
17. Ⓐ Ⓑ Ⓒ Ⓓ	42. Ⓐ Ⓑ Ⓒ Ⓓ
18. Ⓐ Ⓑ Ⓒ Ⓓ	43. Ⓐ Ⓑ Ⓒ Ⓓ
19. Ⓐ Ⓑ Ⓒ Ⓓ	44. Ⓐ Ⓑ Ⓒ Ⓓ
20. Ⓐ Ⓑ Ⓒ Ⓓ	45. Ⓐ Ⓑ Ⓒ Ⓓ
21. Ⓐ Ⓑ Ⓒ Ⓓ	46. Ⓐ Ⓑ Ⓒ Ⓓ
22. Ⓐ Ⓑ Ⓒ Ⓓ	47. Ⓐ Ⓑ Ⓒ Ⓓ
23. Ⓐ Ⓑ Ⓒ Ⓓ	48. Ⓐ Ⓑ Ⓒ Ⓓ
24. Ⓐ Ⓑ Ⓒ Ⓓ	49. Ⓐ Ⓑ Ⓒ Ⓓ
25. Ⓐ Ⓑ Ⓒ Ⓓ	50. Ⓐ Ⓑ Ⓒ Ⓓ

SECTION 2
STRUCTURE AND WRITTEN COMPREHENSION

1. Ⓐ Ⓑ Ⓒ Ⓓ	26. Ⓐ Ⓑ Ⓒ Ⓓ
2. Ⓐ Ⓑ Ⓒ Ⓓ	27. Ⓐ Ⓑ Ⓒ Ⓓ
3. Ⓐ Ⓑ Ⓒ Ⓓ	28. Ⓐ Ⓑ Ⓒ Ⓓ
4. Ⓐ Ⓑ Ⓒ Ⓓ	29. Ⓐ Ⓑ Ⓒ Ⓓ
5. Ⓐ Ⓑ Ⓒ Ⓓ	30. Ⓐ Ⓑ Ⓒ Ⓓ
6. Ⓐ Ⓑ Ⓒ Ⓓ	31. Ⓐ Ⓑ Ⓒ Ⓓ
7. Ⓐ Ⓑ Ⓒ Ⓓ	32. Ⓐ Ⓑ Ⓒ Ⓓ
8. Ⓐ Ⓑ Ⓒ Ⓓ	33. Ⓐ Ⓑ Ⓒ Ⓓ
9. Ⓐ Ⓑ Ⓒ Ⓓ	34. Ⓐ Ⓑ Ⓒ Ⓓ
10. Ⓐ Ⓑ Ⓒ Ⓓ	35. Ⓐ Ⓑ Ⓒ Ⓓ
11. Ⓐ Ⓑ Ⓒ Ⓓ	36. Ⓐ Ⓑ Ⓒ Ⓓ
12. Ⓐ Ⓑ Ⓒ Ⓓ	37. Ⓐ Ⓑ Ⓒ Ⓓ
13. Ⓐ Ⓑ Ⓒ Ⓓ	38. Ⓐ Ⓑ Ⓒ Ⓓ
14. Ⓐ Ⓑ Ⓒ Ⓓ	39. Ⓐ Ⓑ Ⓒ Ⓓ
15. Ⓐ Ⓑ Ⓒ Ⓓ	40. Ⓐ Ⓑ Ⓒ Ⓓ
16. Ⓐ Ⓑ Ⓒ Ⓓ	
17. Ⓐ Ⓑ Ⓒ Ⓓ	
18. Ⓐ Ⓑ Ⓒ Ⓓ	
19. Ⓐ Ⓑ Ⓒ Ⓓ	
20. Ⓐ Ⓑ Ⓒ Ⓓ	
21. Ⓐ Ⓑ Ⓒ Ⓓ	
22. Ⓐ Ⓑ Ⓒ Ⓓ	
23. Ⓐ Ⓑ Ⓒ Ⓓ	
24. Ⓐ Ⓑ Ⓒ Ⓓ	
25. Ⓐ Ⓑ Ⓒ Ⓓ	

SECTION 1
READING COMPREHENSION AND VOCABULARY

1. Ⓐ Ⓑ Ⓒ Ⓓ	26. Ⓐ Ⓑ Ⓒ Ⓓ	51. Ⓐ Ⓑ Ⓒ Ⓓ
2. Ⓐ Ⓑ Ⓒ Ⓓ	27. Ⓐ Ⓑ Ⓒ Ⓓ	52. Ⓐ Ⓑ Ⓒ Ⓓ
3. Ⓐ Ⓑ Ⓒ Ⓓ	28. Ⓐ Ⓑ Ⓒ Ⓓ	53. Ⓐ Ⓑ Ⓒ Ⓓ
4. Ⓐ Ⓑ Ⓒ Ⓓ	29. Ⓐ Ⓑ Ⓒ Ⓓ	54. Ⓐ Ⓑ Ⓒ Ⓓ
5. Ⓐ Ⓑ Ⓒ Ⓓ	30. Ⓐ Ⓑ Ⓒ Ⓓ	55. Ⓐ Ⓑ Ⓒ Ⓓ
6. Ⓐ Ⓑ Ⓒ Ⓓ	31. Ⓐ Ⓑ Ⓒ Ⓓ	56. Ⓐ Ⓑ Ⓒ Ⓓ
7. Ⓐ Ⓑ Ⓒ Ⓓ	32. Ⓐ Ⓑ Ⓒ Ⓓ	57. Ⓐ Ⓑ Ⓒ Ⓓ
8. Ⓐ Ⓑ Ⓒ Ⓓ	33. Ⓐ Ⓑ Ⓒ Ⓓ	58. Ⓐ Ⓑ Ⓒ Ⓓ
9. Ⓐ Ⓑ Ⓒ Ⓓ	34. Ⓐ Ⓑ Ⓒ Ⓓ	59. Ⓐ Ⓑ Ⓒ Ⓓ
10. Ⓐ Ⓑ Ⓒ Ⓓ	35. Ⓐ Ⓑ Ⓒ Ⓓ	60. Ⓐ Ⓑ Ⓒ Ⓓ
11. Ⓐ Ⓑ Ⓒ Ⓓ	36. Ⓐ Ⓑ Ⓒ Ⓓ	
12. Ⓐ Ⓑ Ⓒ Ⓓ	37. Ⓐ Ⓑ Ⓒ Ⓓ	
13. Ⓐ Ⓑ Ⓒ Ⓓ	38. Ⓐ Ⓑ Ⓒ Ⓓ	
14. Ⓐ Ⓑ Ⓒ Ⓓ	39. Ⓐ Ⓑ Ⓒ Ⓓ	
15. Ⓐ Ⓑ Ⓒ Ⓓ	40. Ⓐ Ⓑ Ⓒ Ⓓ	
16. Ⓐ Ⓑ Ⓒ Ⓓ	41. Ⓐ Ⓑ Ⓒ Ⓓ	
17. Ⓐ Ⓑ Ⓒ Ⓓ	42. Ⓐ Ⓑ Ⓒ Ⓓ	
18. Ⓐ Ⓑ Ⓒ Ⓓ	43. Ⓐ Ⓑ Ⓒ Ⓓ	
19. Ⓐ Ⓑ Ⓒ Ⓓ	44. Ⓐ Ⓑ Ⓒ Ⓓ	
20. Ⓐ Ⓑ Ⓒ Ⓓ	45. Ⓐ Ⓑ Ⓒ Ⓓ	
21. Ⓐ Ⓑ Ⓒ Ⓓ	46. Ⓐ Ⓑ Ⓒ Ⓓ	
22. Ⓐ Ⓑ Ⓒ Ⓓ	47. Ⓐ Ⓑ Ⓒ Ⓓ	
23. Ⓐ Ⓑ Ⓒ Ⓓ	48. Ⓐ Ⓑ Ⓒ Ⓓ	
24. Ⓐ Ⓑ Ⓒ Ⓓ	49. Ⓐ Ⓑ Ⓒ Ⓓ	
25. Ⓐ Ⓑ Ⓒ Ⓓ	50. Ⓐ Ⓑ Ⓒ Ⓓ	

Answer Sheet for Practice Test 4

Tear this sheet out and use it to mark your answers.

SECTION 1
LISTENING
COMPREHENSION

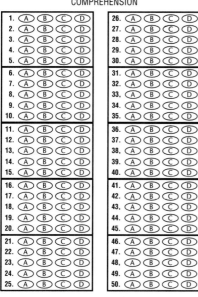

SECTION 2
STRUCTURE AND
WRITTEN COMPREHENSION

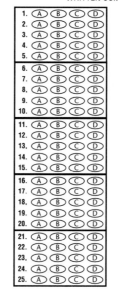

SECTION 1
READING COMPREHENSION
AND VOCABULARY

Personal Study Plan

Listening Targets	Practice Tests			
STATEMENTS	1	2	3	4
Similar Sounds				
Number Discrimination				
Synonyms				
Negation				
Contextual Reference				
Cause and Effect				
Conditionals				
Chronological Order				
Comparisons				
SHORT DIALOGS				
Similar Sounds				
Number Discrimination				
Synonyms				
Negation				
Contextual Reference				
Cause and Effect				
Conditionals				
Chronological Order				
Comparisons				
MINI-TALKS				
Mini-Talks				
Dialogs				

Structure Targets

Structure	1	2	3	4
Subject Omitted				
Subject Repeated				
Verb Omitted				
Verb: Unnecessary Form				
Verb: Inappropriate Tense				
Verb: Subject-Verb Agreement				
Articles				
Word Order: Subject-Verb				
W/O: Adjective/Adverb Placement				
Pronouns: Agreement				
Pronouns: Form				
Prepositions				
Noun Clauses				
Adjective Clauses				
Adverb Clauses				
Reduced Adjective Clauses				
Reduced Adverb Clauses				
Parallel Structures				
Gerunds and Infinitives				
Participle Form				
Conditionals				
Comparisons				
Subjunctive				
Word Families				
Active/Passive Verbs				